FREEDOM FROM RELIGION

Past Shock Part Three

Jack Barranger

The Book Tree
San Diego, California

Freedom From Religion
Past Shock Part Three

© 2008
by Jack Barranger

ISBN 978-1-58509-116-4

Editor: Kimberly Dillon
Cover layout & design: Daniel Flood

Published by
The Book Tree
P O Box 16476
San Diego, CA 92176
www.thebooktree.com

We provide fascinating and educational products to help awaken the public to new ideas and information that would not be available otherwise.
Call 1 (800) 700-8733 for our *FREE BOOK TREE CATALOG*.

To Dietrich Bonhoeffer

CONTENTS

Introduction

WARNING!
Forewarned is Forearmed

Beware: reading this book could set you free. For all of your life, you have been carrying around a slave chip that states, "Thou Shalt Be a Slave." This slave chip in physical terms weighs nothing, yet in your life it weighs you down more than anything in your life experience.

The slave chip is an ancient programming. Most people consider this ancient programming to be a natural part of their life experience. There is nothing natural about this programming, and it is robbing people of having a rich life experience.

Imagine seeing someone struggling to carry a large suitcase full of rocks. It weighs him down and the strain that it is putting on him is quite obvious. You feel compassion for the person, and you ask him why he is carrying such a heavy load. He responds in a way which shocks you.

"You don't understand. These rocks are me. Every one of them is something sacred. I would be nothing without these rocks."

You look inside the suitcase and notice that some of the rocks are rather large. Without your asking, the rock carrier begins explaining the rocks.

"This is the 'noble slavery' rock. This rock enables me to do things I don't want to do and feel good about it. It's really heavy, but it makes me feel good."

"This is the 'delay' rock. With this rock I don't have to experience anything good in the present. I can put off fulfilling and satisfactory life experiences as long as I want. This rock helps me feel good about something I haven't experienced yet."

"This is the 'poverty' rock. This rock helps me feel good about not having the money and passion to do things I would really like to do. With this rock I can feel spiritual about not being able to travel or not being able to afford some of the things that at one time were mighty dreams in my life."

"This is the 'humility' rock. This aids me in accepting that I can't live up to some of the dreams I had for my life. It helps me feel safe and aids me in giving up things I would really like to have and experience."

Then the person takes a few of the smaller stones and sets them beside the suitcase.

"These are a bunch of my belief rocks."

"This one helps me to embrace the idea that I'm not good enough to accomplish some of my dreams. It's a good rock: it keeps me from getting into trouble. It also keeps me from moving into areas that would make me depressed if I didn't succeed."

"This little thing helps me feel good about going to work every day in a job which I really don't find that exciting. However, this rock helps me realize that work is noble and that even if I don't like what I'm doing, I'm still worthy because I'm doing it."

"Here's a nice one. If I start having thoughts which suggest that I could experience a better life, this one stops me right in my tracks. It keeps me in place and prevents my thinking about things which may be beyond my talents."

"And look at this one. This one helps me to feel good about myself because I am living in the right country and have values which are superior to people who live in other countries. I don't know what I'd do without this rock."

My bearer of rocks picks up a big one and gleams with pride.

"This is one of my favorites. This is the 'right stuff spiritual' rock. This one really makes me feel good because it makes me aware that I am one of the few fortunate people on this planet to be a member of the one true religion. When all these other rocks are weighing me down, this rock gives me strength because I know that my beliefs are the correct beliefs. I really feel sorry for people who are not fortunate enough to have this rock."

I cannot hide my sadness, and finally ask, "Instead of having a rock that makes you feel good about all the other rocks, why don't you just dump all the rocks and walk more freely?"

This person is stunned.

"You're really messed up, you know that. You don't know how valuable all these rocks are to me. These rocks are sacred. What kind of person are you to tell me that I should dump all these rocks? You're evil!"

Quickly, the young man throws all the rocks into his suitcase and walks off quickly. The strain of the load is very obvious – especially when he is trying to get away from the one person who could begin in him the process of liberation. As he is walking away, he is heard to state, "Lord, protect me from those who do not see the value in these rocks."

As ridiculous as this story sounds, it is true of everyone on this planet. Every person carries an ancient programming which is referred to in this book as the SLAVE CHIP. Like a computer chip, it does what a programmer programmed it to do. It cannot think for itself, yet it can really get in the way of people who want to think for themselves. This slave chip is so effective that people who follow its' dictates actually believe that they are thinking for themselves. They never question the dictates of this slave chip because they have not learned how to draw a distinction between the leanings of their own souls and the programming which prevents people from experiencing the voice of their own souls.

Thus, this book is issuing a warning.

If you begin looking at your ancient conditioning, the experience may not be pleasant, but it will begin the process of liberating you.

As you begin to release yourself from the programming of the slave chip, the slave chip's own mechanisms will kick in and send you messages to stop and return to your slave mode.

Inside of you is a part of you that does not want you free. It will fight to keep you in a state of slavery, and it does this by keeping your slave chip intact. This slave chip is not a creative mechanism. It was programmed into you long ago by ancient "gods" that wanted humans as a worker race rather than the creative and powerful beings they were capable of being.

While these beings are no longer here, their programming has created a slave chip which lingers with us with devastating power.

(This controversial thesis is no longer considered that "way out." Writers like Zecheria Sitchin, Neil Freer, William Bramley, and Rene Boulay have each written extensively on the thesis that humans were created as a slave race thousands of years ago. I joined these writers with my book *Past Shock*, promoting the thesis that the gods of the past were historical rather than mythological. These gods treated their human creations very badly, and we are still reeling from events which happened thousands of years ago. One of the most egregious acts they did to us was the creation of a programming which was so powerful that it still impacts us today. For those wanting more background on this controversial thesis, a short summary of my book *Past Shock* is in "Appendix A.")

This slave chip causes us to come up far short of what we can be as human beings. It "inspires" us to do things we don't really want to do. It "helps" us feel bad when we feel a surge of possibility from the realm of the soul. When we have these visions, the slave chip kicks in and makes us feel silly and unworthy. The slave chip is not our friend, yet it portrays itself as a worthy ally. It keeps us in hell, when we are capable of soaring in heavenly places.

So, why the warning?

This slave chip is programmed to protect itself. It is like a terrorist bomb that will blow up if a bomb squad person dares to tamper with it. However, the bomb squad expert can save lives if it operates carefully and diffuses it.

The analogy holds with your slave chip. The slave chip does not want to be diffused. It wants to keep operating in the same harmful way it has been doing throughout your life. Daring to question its programmed values could cause it to get mean. This is true of life: some people get mean when others start to get free.

That's the bad news.

The good news is that this programming can be overcome. That's the purpose of this book. People who get mean when you want to break free only have power to the degree that you give it to them. Realizing exactly what they are doing reduces their power significantly. Realizing the price of wanting these people's approval is an epiphany which is part of the process of liberation. The good news is that this slave chip is powerful only to the degree that you give it power.

This slave chip can be deprogrammed.

The slave chip will fight and use every means to keep itself intact. It can create guilt, feelings of unworthiness, despair, and a sense that you are walking down the wrong path. While these surges of programming may not feel good, they are your best indication that you are walking on the right path.

In so many ways the slave chip is an amazing piece of work. It has helped you to feel good about things which were not good for you. It has helped you to feel bad about things that could change your life significantly for the better. It has led you to believe that your dreams are silly and impossible. It has helped you remain in a life which is significantly limited in possibility, and it has helped you feel that this is more noble, more real, and more acceptable than the possibilities of your life which are waiting to be explored.

The slave chip wants you shut down.

The slave chip wants you working hard for things that are not really worth having.

The slave chip wants you to be a shell of yourself.

Your slave chip wants you to remain a slave. That's what it was created for: to keep you locked in slavery. For most people the slave chip has shut people down and guided them to a life which falls fall short of their potential. This is what it wants to do with you. If you mess with that, it will fight to keep you limited and unfulfilled. That is what it is programmed to do. It is not evil. However, it is well constructed and does its job well.

With increasing numbers of people on this planet, this is going to change for some of them.

Why don't you be one of them?

Chapter One

What Is the Slave Chip?

The slave chip is not anything new. It has been with us for thousands of years. It is a programming deep within all of us that moves us in directions that are not in our best interests. The slave chip is the result of ancient conditioning. Thousands of years ago controlling forces did not have our best interests in mind. Instead, these forces needed humans who would bend to their will with as little resistance as possible.

However, the ancient humans did not bend to the will of these "gods" quickly enough. Many rebelled and refused to do the will of the ancient gods. Therefore, a drastic move was needed to insure that humans would do what they were told without questioning authority or wanting to know why such slavery was being inflicted upon them.

In my book *Past Shock*, I do a synthesis of many writers who wrote about the ancient past. This is my third book in what I term a "freedom from religion" series. These books tell you (1) how religion was formed, (2) how it is impacting us today, and finally (3) how we can get free of religion. The ancient past was not a pretty time. It was a series of shocks from which we have not yet recovered. These gods, referred to as "pretender gods" in *Past Shock*, desperately needed a worker race to prevent a mutiny among their own race. After much deliberation, they decided to create one. Thus began the human race as we know it today.

No doubt our souls were created by the true God to be free and full of joy. Unfortunately, the pretender gods did not have freedom and abundance on their agenda for their newly created humans. Their agenda included obedient slaves who would work hard without complaint or resistance.

However, it didn't happen that way. The newly created humans were very bright and didn't take well to the menial work expected of them by these pretender gods. Thus, they kept experimenting until they found a way to have humans work hard without complaining. This meant dumbing humans down to the point where they accepted their highly limited lot without complaining. Evidently, they found a way to program humans in such a manner that we would not only accept our highly limiting lives, but also that we would inflict this limiting lifestyle on others.

This is the slave chip – like a chip inside a computer. After all, our brain is a computer, and, unfortunetely, it is easily programmed. It was more easily programmed when technologically advanced "gods" programmed us.

The slave chip is a very intricate web of programming that keeps people locked into being far less than they are capable of being. It kicks in when people want to break free. It causes doubt when the human soul sends visions of what life can be like. It provides mental barriers to people who want to move to higher levels of life expression.

The slave chip is both individual and collective.

Individually, each person has his or her unique programming from life experience. Some believe that this unique programming might even extend back into previous lives. This may or may not be true. However, it makes a mighty devastating impact whether coming just from this life or from many alleged lives that we may have experienced before.

However, it is the collective slave chip that impacts the individual slave chip. This collective slave chip results from social and cultural conditioning. This less obvious conditioning sets up the expectations that cultures and societies have for people living within their structures. Different cultures have different expectations of their citizens. However, all of these expectations from different cultures have one thing in common: they want to limit the manner in which you choose to live your life. Put another way, they want you to live in more of a slavery mode than a freedom mode.

One of the most ironic parts of this slave chip is that it will look with disdain upon other cultural programming. People in the United States will see Islamic women as oppressed and fail to see the oppression of women in this country. People in other countries will see America as the Great Satan, and fail to see to see any "Satanic mores" in their own eyes that need to be cast out.

The slave chip is so effective in its programming that it can convince people that they are becoming more free while they are actually inflicting themselves with a greater slavery. Many people experience a sense of liberation with a religious conversion experience. Yet lying in the wings of various religions are billions of people with very strong slave chips. They see the projection of their own slavery onto others as something that will liberate people.

The slave chip's programming is so effective that it will see a limiting life as noble, and a freer life as irresponsible. These modes of conditioning are powerful. They are never the result of original thought. Instead, they are fragments passed down from the collective slave chip and embraced as truth. Working hard rather than working smart is seen as the way to go. That is the dictum of the slave chip. Giving up something in order to get something is seen as noble, despite the fact that ways exist that do not require anyone to lose anything. Feeling the need to delay fulfillment until it is earned is one of the greatest victories of the slave chip. It does its job very well.

I am a retired college teacher. If it were not for millions of people programmed to go to college, I would not have had a job. The collective slave chip kept me employed. It insures that few people will question whether any real value comes from a college education. Following the dictates of the slave chip's programming, people will simply enroll in colleges all over the United States. That is what their programming, their parents' programming, and society's programming urge young people to do. What is so amazing is that this slave chip programming is very powerful. Many college-age people don't even question whether this is their best move. Many think of it as their only move.

Those who genuinely do question the value of a college education are seen as being "out of the swim." This is where the slave chip does its job so well. It causes people to doubt whether their own doubts are legitimate. Doubt that a certain religion is not the true religion, and guilt will ensue. It doesn't matter what the religion is. The slave chip works effectively for all religions and much of life.

Question the values you were programmed to have, and your slave chip will help you feel bad. With its powerful conditioning, it will help stop your process of original thinking. It will then drive you back to values that keep you enslaved within a highly limited paradigm. It will also cause you to work even harder to retain your conditioning. You may move into some original thinking that will help you break free of your slave chip conditioning. Then you will experience doubt, frustration, and guilt. Your slave chip is not creative. However, it will kick in when you dare to get creative with your life.

Your slave chip is like a well-programmed computer chip. It is very intricate and very sophisticated. Like the computer chip, it is programmed to keep you a slave. Just as one cannot run a new program on a old embedded computer chip, it is very difficult to run a freedom program on a slave chip. This is especially true when the slave chip has its own limited ideas about what freedom is.

We were close to experiencing a Y2K disaster. Some claimed that it would be a complete catastrophe. Others claimed that it was going to be very troublesome. Others thought it would not be the disaster that some claimed it would be. The problem was solved because millions of lines of programming were rewritten to replace 00 with 2000. (With the simple two digit 00, computers would have read the year as 1900, and this could have caused all sorts of problems.)

The bottom line, from nearly everyone's viewpoint, was that some serious reprogramming was essential.

The same is true if we begin living lives based on freedom programming rather than slavery programming. That will happen when people begin deprogramming their slave chips. They will begin experiencing more freedom and less or no slavery. This takes work, but the payoff far exceeds the effort.

The slave chip is not physical. It cannot be rooted out as the result of a surgical operation. Nor can it be overcome by writing positive-thinking affirmations alone. The act of writing dozens of affirmations a day is more an act of slavery than an act of freedom. Yet mainly, in new thought and new age circles, the act of writing and speaking affirmations is considered to be a fruitful act. Sadly, it rarely is. It does not address the unconscious issues generated by the slave chip. Instead, it keeps on sending out its own messages of limitation:

You're not good enough to do that.

You're going to have to work hard to get that.

You're not mature enough to do that.

You want to do what?

Just accept your lot in life. That's what good people do.

That's a real immature thought.

The slave chip keeps people looking outside of themselves for the joys they experience. It keeps people locked into getting their main joy from watching things like Barry Bonds becoming the all-time home run leader. Nothing is wrong with this. However, for many, this passive act replaces people hitting "home runs" in their own lives. Instead of being in a career that is so fulfilling that they virtually touch all of the bases, people are "inspired" to get their main satisfaction from vicarious experiences.

What does this have to do with the slave chip?

Too many people passively watch a great sports event that provides them with more pleasure than anything they themselves did that week. (There is nothing wrong with this; I am a great sports fan myself, but when this becomes your main source of pleasure, you might be more addicted to the slave chip than you realize.) People locked up in the programming of the slave chip get more joy from seeing others do things. This can prevent them from doing mighty things in their own lives. This is one of the greatest victories of the slave chip. It "inspires" us to look outside of ourselves for the things that are really meaningful and fulfilling in life.

A person might feel guilty or in danger when she stands up to the programming of the slave chip. However, the slave chip is so effective that it will generate a "feel-bad" program when you dare to stand up to its devastating programming. No one other than your own soul cheers when you begin standing up to your slave chip programming. However, the collective slave chip is so powerful that most people will not cheer when you start deprogramming it. You may even feel threatened when you start breaking for freedom.

The collective slave chip is very powerful. You will not be able to change it. It is firmly entrenched within all societies and cultures. It dominates so effectively that people collectively are not even going to confront it. Your way to freedom and a more fulfilling and successful life is to deprogram your own slave chip.

Only when increasing numbers of people begin deprogramming their own slave chips will people begin experiencing freedom on a more collective level. I doubt very much if this is going to happen anytime soon. Instead, we appear to be going in the opposite direction. Collectively, people are limiting their own freedoms. In a 1997 poll, 70% of Americans surveyed claimed that they would be willing to give up a majority of the freedoms stated in the Constitution's Bill of Rights to be more secure. (The Patriot Act, which came a few years later, is an excellent example of that.) Some cracks in the wall of slavery are noticed by a few who then realize that the walls should crumble. However, the majority of people rush in with sealant to prevent any further cracking. These people are not mean or evil. They are just very well-programmed.

So are all of us. However, we don't have to let that continue. Once we become aware of the slave chip and its programming, we can rush toward our goals with minimal programmed resistance. You can reduce the slave chip's power and eventually shut it off.

When this happens, life achieves a greater flow and joy. Impossible goals now seem possible with far less struggle. The willingness to experience joy instead of struggle begins to dominate. The success that you achieve is done with much less effort and more meaningful results. Your life becomes richer and more meaningful. You move more deeply into the natural condition of your own soul's leading. This is the way life is meant to be lived. This is our natural condition.

Standing in the way of this is your individual slave chip, which is the result of thousands of years of ancient conditioning. Deprogramming that slave chip is just about the sanest thing you could do in this lifetime.

Chapter Two

How the Slave Chip Works

Think about things that we do automatically. Most people feel the urge to cheer when a baseball player hits a home run. This runs the gamut from professional baseball right down to parents watching their son in a sandlot game. The response is automatic.

This next part is going to sound silly, but bear with me. Rarely will the fan or the parents feel compassion for the pitcher who gave up the home run ball. We have been programmed from birth to cheer for winners, and having feelings ranging from neutral to disgust for people who lose. This may be the first home run the pitcher has given up in weeks and his earned run average may be a phenomenal 2.11 (meaning that he has only given up slightly more than two runs for each nine innings pitched). However, if one of those runs is the winning run, the pitcher is seen as a loser, despite doing a terrific job overall.

Our programming is very strong in many areas. A student could have learned a lot in a class and received a "B." Another student taking the same course with a much easier teacher gets an "A." However, this person has little knowledge or skill to show for it. The letter grade is seen as more important than the actual knowledge. Society's values have programmed us from our very early years to go for the grade. This happens often at the expense of useful knowledge.

Programming and conditioning are powerful forces. They cause us to do things that may actually limit our experiencing the fullness of life. Conditioning will aid a person in selecting a career based on what other people think rather than basing that career on something he would love to do. Conditioning will also heavily influence a person to choose a career based more on how much she is paid. Seeking fulfillment in her work is not in her programming. Sometimes this conditioning is so powerful that the process of conscious thought isn't even involved.

The Slave Chip – An Unconscious Force

The slave chip is not some vile and evil force attempting to prevent you from experiencing the fullness of life. It is instead the fallout from an ancient programming. This programming and conditioning began thousands of years ago. The beings who programmed and conditioned us are no longer here. However, their conditioning lingers with devastating impact.

The slave chip worked back then because the programming and conditioning was very effective.

The slave chip continues to work today because few people have the courage to challenge the programming and conditioning.

A good example from the past is the building and tearing down of the Tower of Babel. According to Zecharia Sitchin, this was a highly creative act done by very intelligent humans. They were attempting to escape their slave masters. What this *wasn't* was a group of stupid people who decided to build a high tower so that they could reach God. Instead, this was a group of brilliant humans who so wanted to reach the true God that they built something that could remove them from the planet. (Zecharia Sitchin in *The Twelfth Planet* claims these early humans were building a spaceship to get to the gods' planet Nibiru to protest how they were being treated. Not one of the gods was following the "prime directive" – a policy of non-intervention, so we could learn and evolve on our own.)

As you probably know, the Tower of Babel story has a tragic ending. The tower was destroyed. Moreover, the gods determined that the human species had to be dumbed down. The edict, "Let us go down and confound their language" came as a result of the humans becoming too smart for their own good. At least that was the view of the gods. Thus, a stronger programming and conditioning was instituted. That programming was the beginning of religion.

Many people reading about the Tower of Babel simply believe that the humans were arrogant and deserved what they got. We can thank organized religion for that view. However, anyone reading the account in Genesis 11 who truly thinks about it can see a different story. If we read it apart from the conditioning of the slave chip, we see something amazing: we were becoming like the gods. Keep in mind the fact that history is written by winners. You will then see the events for what they are, and a sober reality emerges. The arrogant ones were not the humans. The arrogant ones were the petty gods. They feared that the human race was becoming too intelligent for its own good.

These arrogant gods were the ones who created the slave chip. Their conditioning is so effective that this act of overt spiritual terrorism is seen as necessary and just.

As a young boy, I bought into the conditioning. How dare those humans think that they could climb that high and find God. The conditioning was nearly total. It never occurred to me that if God was indeed on planet Earth at the time, why did people need to build a tower (or spaceship) to find "Him."

Just putting the word "him" in quotes will touch on some people's conditioning. Colleagues of mine have had students officially complain when a teacher refers to God as "She." This is slave chip conditioning at its worst. The view of a patriarchal God is a relatively new concept in human history. Yet some people can only relate to a God who is male.

I get the same conditioned response from my feminist students when I claim that the devil is a "she." The conditioning is embedded in these "liberated" people. While God could be a she, the devil is definitely male. At least that is the concensus reality of just about all of humanity.

This is how the slave chip works. It fires off values to us that are based on conditioning more than experience.

In America, when I open a door for a woman, she will usually express gratitude.

In Denmark (where I lived for a year), when I opened doors for women, many were insulted. I learned this the hard way. However, it taught me a lot about conditioning.

The slave chip works to limit us. It has been programmed to have us be slaves. This programming is so effective that when someone tries to break free of slavery, the slave chip actually attempts to stop the effort. The slave chip never uses words. It actually "creates" strong feelings that would say the following, if translated into words:

Who do you think you are?

You went too far that time.

Face reality!

If you keep this up, your soul is in danger.

The irony of this last comment is that the soul is the force within everyone urging people to break free. The ego is in conjunction with the slave chip conditioning. It urges people to shut themselves down in any quest for personal freedom.

The slave chip works because thousands of years ago it was honed to perfection. Humans who didn't want to do menial work were conditioned to think that their work was noble, even holy. The Garden of Eden experience conditions people to think that they must work by the sweat of their brow and struggle in that effort. This happened as a result of the "mistake" that Adam and Eve made thousands of years ago. Eve got to experience pain in childbirth for the same "sin." At least that is what we are told.

The slave chip works very effectively in helping humans to think that Adam and Eve had it coming. That same conditioning helps people in the western world to think that the serpent was evil. Yet anyone who reads the story closely will quickly realize that "God" was lying. It was actually the serpent who was telling the truth. (God said that Adam and Eve would die from eating from the tree of knowledge. In fact, Adam and Eve were told they would die even if they touched the tree. The serpent, in contrast, said that both would see as clearly as the gods. The serpent had our best interests in mind.)

In modern life, the slave chip works very effectively in leading us to believe that we are limited human beings. Being seen as a fallen creature, thanks to the deeds of two people, doesn't help. When the true God attempts to inspire people to move beyond their limitations, the slave chip sends up "barrier thoughts" to halt the process of liberation.

This happens in different ways with different people. Just as a good word processing program has a search and find feature, so does the slave chip. With no real thought, it simply goes for a weak area and works there.

For some, that would be sending feelings that one is not worthy enough, educated enough, or committed enough to accomplish an inspired life goal.

For others, it would urge them to worry about what others would think. The fear of loss of acceptance is intensified to the point of discouraging the recently inspired person.

Some will experience a form of conditioning that claims that if we suffer in this life, we will be rewarded in the next life. This really worked well in ancient times to get people to do work they hated to do.

For others, the slave chip will create good feelings about sacrificing oneself for someone else in order to feel "spiritual." For my book *Knowing When to Quit*, I interviewed more than 400 people. Many of them felt that they were stuck in terrible circumstances because they were sinful creatures. Others felt that they did something in a previous life that necessitated being miserable in this life to work off karma. The slave chip doesn't care whether you are Hindu, Jewish, or Christian. It will find the weak spot and use any present conditioning to take you back to following an ancient conditioning.

Constantly attempting to keep you enslaved, the slave chip is even capable of generating good feelings about things that simply aren't good for you. You want to travel before you settle down in a job, but your conditioning – and the conditioning of others – is to start the job right after college. You may have bad feelings about an upcoming marriage, but the invitations have been sent out and you are strongly conditioned not to look selfish. Despite valid evidence that this marriage may not be a good idea, well-meaning people step forward saying, "Everybody gets the pre-wedding jitters." In some future time, you may step up and say the same thing to someone else.

The personal slave chip works in synergetic tandem with the collective slave chip. The ancient conditioning has been with us for thousands of years. However, our own unique cultural conditioning leads us from this conditioning and reinforces it. For some it is the most devastating aspects of the Puritan work ethic. With this, work is seen as a glorious end in itself. Thoughts of fulfillment, personal satisfaction, and doing what one loves to do are not part of the programming. The programming simply says: "Work hard, and you will be worthy."

For others, the individual and the collective slave chips work together to produce a devastating "wait until later" syndrome. In *Knowing When to Quit*, I referred to this as the "staying syndrome." The conditioning here "inspires" people to delay their freedom and their fulfillment until some future time. Its ugly head is reared in the idea that one must earn fulfillment instead of embracing it. If one actually gets to do what she loves to do, the conditioning claims that this will take time, dedication, and patience. This goes contrary to the leanings of the soul, which claims that acts should be free now, and that freedom never costs anything.

For still others, the conditioning from the collective and individual slave chips combines with the lower side of organized religion. It claims that we are unworthy creatures. It is very hard for anyone to embrace a free and richly rewarding life if she thinks that she is not worthy. Another aspect of this is accepting that God has said no to the desire to have a satisfying life based on doing what one loves to do. The slave chip conditioning helps people to accept what the very soul of a person would find unacceptable.

A promotion to a more stressful work-style is accepted because the slave chip, along with the ego, claims that this is the right thing to do.

A toxic relationship remains toxic because the slave chip claims that the relationship as an end in itself is more important than the happiness of the two people involved in the relationship.

A desire to try something new is squashed by the slave chip's conditioning, because so much time and effort has been "invested" in the old way of life.

The desire to move to a new level of personal freedom is squelched because the slave chip, in league with the ego, sends out messages that such a move is inappropriate, immature, and lacking in sound judgment.

The slave chip works very well because it is extremely consistent. What will liberate you will be felt as bad; what will keep you enslaved will be felt as good. This conditioning and the ego that uses it are very adept at what they do.

Chapter Three

The Slave Chip in Modern Society

Individual people can shake off the effects of the slave chip. However, it is almost impossible for entire societies to de-program their group slave chips. People collectively do not want to face their own demons. Yet, individual people are willing to face their demons when they realize what the cost is of ignoring them.

Despite all the political and religious rhetoric, societies are not evil. I learned this very quickly when I spent two weeks in East Germany less than three years after the Berlin wall was erected. I was highly conditioned about East Germany. I thought that I would find radically different people – people enslaved by the "evils" of communism. What I found instead were people just like the people I associated with in America. A few were boorish; most were very humane.

I spoke with soldiers guarding the border. A couple of them told me that they intentionally missed when they were shooting at people trying to escape. When I rode through East Germany on their trains, conductors would quietly tell me that they looked forward to the day when the two Germanys would be united again. People sensing that I was lost walked up to help me. One of these people was a woman who had not seen or heard from her West Berlin son in three years. She asked me to deliver a letter to him.

These experiences obliterated my safe societal conditioning. These "commies" were real people whom I liked. They had dreams like mine. They loved their children. They felt a pride when East Germans began doing well in Olympic events. Eventually, they even helped break down the Berlin wall.

My society was not evil for conditioning me to think this way. It simply was following its own slave chip conditioning. I saw others enslaved while failing to recognize my own lack of real freedom.

My conditioning came crashing down because my own experiences would not support it. This is exactly what will happen in your life. If you embrace experience over belief, the power of your conditioning will begin to whither.

In society, the slave chip works very effectively. Few people are aware of it. Even fewer people dare to challenge it.

Thus, the collective slave chip reigns with a lot of power. In what ways does it impact us in modern society?

One of the main areas where this conditioning is felt is in the nation's schools. Real education is not really the priority of the schools. The impact of the collective slave chip shows up in the fact that schools are much better at indoctrinating than they are at educating. Schools don't teach people *how* to think as much as they tell people *what* to think. In this way, education is a pawn of the slave chip rather than a means of helping people to get free of it.

Just as in ancient times, the teacher is seen as the final authority. While some noble teachers do teach students how to think for themselves, most teachers are more comfortable getting students to think what they want them to think. Wittingly or unwittingly, they pass on their own conditioning:

> If you want to be something in life, you are going to have to go to college.

> People who make a lot of money are more important than those who create works of art.

> Athletes are models for what is good in society.

Fitting in is much more important than living life according to your vision.

Looking good is much more important than living freely.

I was an educator for thirty-seven years. I totally agree with the educational critics who claim that America's schools do a better job of creating slaves than creating effective people. As a college teacher, I watched visionary college freshmen turn into cynical sophomores in one to two years. Nothing in the college curriculum aids people in embracing a satisfying and meaningful life. Instead, much in the college experience actually blocked people from achieving these goals.

The awesome force of organized religion in America has aided the slave chip in impacting people's lives in a negative way. The subtitle of my book *Past Shock* was *The Origin of Religion and Its Impact on the Human Soul*. (I eventually used this sub-title for the sequel to *Past Shock*. As I mentioned before, you can learn more about what is in the book *Past Shock* by going to Appendix A.) The original subtitle had the word "devastating" in front of "impact." Yet my publisher and I agreed that because of people's conditioning about the value of religion, the word "devastating" might have been too strong. The word "devastating" was not removed because the word was wrong. It was removed because Americans are highly conditioned to believe that their religions are completely true and real – even if their experiences with it demonstrate otherwise.

Just for contrast, you might be interested to know that only one in ten people believe in God in Poland. In Hungary, the number is only one in seven. America is second in the world with 63% believing in God, fewer only than the Philippines.

(I do not discount the millions of people who have had generally good experiences with religion. The word "experience" is a key word throughout this book. However, all of my "freedom from religion" series books point out how conditioned beliefs can actually hinder the flow of God in people's lives. Religion is often based on ancient conditioning about God rather than a real experience of God. This is almost always counterproductive.)

The slave chip can work through religion in a way that is horrifying. People can be conditioned to believe that having a belief in God is more important than experiencing God. Many actually believe that it is more edifying to read "the word of God" written thousands of years ago than it is to hear the voice for God in their own lives. A majority of Americans actually believe that a loving God would send people to hell for eternity. All of these concepts do not come from truth – or God. They come from intensive conditioning that requires frequent reinforcement.

Issues like prayer in schools and the inflicting of religious morality on a secular society are the results of highly conditioned people. They want their conditioning to be a part of everyone's conditioning. Free will is seen as something to be given lip service. Those who dare to express their free will in ways outside the spiritually correct paradigm will endure the wrath of the self-righteous. There was a saying in the 1960's that the only thing a non-conformist hates worse than a conformist is another non-conformist who won't conform to the prevailing standards of non-conformity.

A famous male movie star made a comment that pointed out conditioning very effectively. In an interview about the new ratings system, he said, "If you show a man biting off a woman's breast, that will get a PG rating; however, if you show a man kissing a woman's breast, that will get you an NC17 rating."

The great concern about the "lower standards" in films shows up in ways that defy logic. Showing a man kicking a man to death will only result in a PG13 rating. However, showing his penis will get an automatic NC17 rating. Logic tells us that being kicked to death is much more horrendous than seeing someone expose himself. However, it is conditioning and ancient programming that rules.

Actually, the movies themselves aid in exacerbating the impact of the slave chip. Movies make people feel good about fitting in. Rarely are people outside the current society's paradigm shown as being heroes. Those who don't fit in are diminished in value. An artist can be portrayed as a hero only if he is dead and had a tragic life. If 50's singer Frankie Lyman had never had a drug problem, no one would have been inspired to make the 1998 film *Why Do Fools Fall in Love*.

A survey of recent films reveals that they contain a certain type of character who is heroic in a way that we have been conditioned to accept. A film about a doctor turned on by the prospect of curing a disease hasn't a chance, yet a film about an outbreak of disease provides good escape – and good conditioning. The heroes – and villains – in the film *Outbreak* were larger than life. This conditions people to think that they cannot live up to this conditioned heroic level.

In my literature classes, when I was teaching poetry, the discussions would eventually turn to love. When I asked, "Where have you seen the greatest love?," many students would refer to the 1997 film *Titanic*. The characters of Jack and Rose in *Titanic* are also larger than life. Only in a movie would a high-society British girl like Rose be swept off her feet by a penniless artist like Jack. Those characters had to be created to "make the movie more easily assimilated by the public." I really enjoyed *Titanic*. It was a damn good story. However, as a student of the slave chip and what it does, I also realize what harm can come from movies like these.

The slave chip wins because "heroic" films enable – and eventually condition – people to look outside of themselves for a sense of meaning. By doing this, a person rubs up more frequently with disappointment. They cannot see a nobility or freedom in their own lives. Constantly rubbing up against disappointment conditions people to settle for less when they are capable of so much more.

Chapter Four

Is Religion Harmful?

THE AUTHOR'S BACKGROUND AND QUALIFICATIONS

I am qualified to write on this subject for a number of reasons. First, I have a theological degree from Gordon-Conwell Theological Institute – a rock solid, Bible-believing fundamentalist Christian seminary. I have spent much of my life as a leader of Christian groups ranging from Young Life to four different youth fellowship groups. In addition to my voluminous reading in seminary, I have also read deeply in the areas of sociology, anthropology, philosophy, history, and physics. With my minimal exposure to other religions in seminary, I have followed through on my own and read most of the holy books of the other world religions.

The more I read about Buddhism and quantum physics, the more I am amazed at how close the Bo tree revelations of Gautama Siddhartha and the latest discoveries of physics are linked. The more I read about archaeological discoveries, the more I realize that the gods and heroes mentioned in mythology are actually historical characters. I increasingly realize the absurdity of claiming that Jehovah and Moses were real life people, but that Zeus and Odysseus were simply figments of a blind poet's imagination. Further study of recently discovered ancient epics begs us to consider that Zeus, Jehovah, and Enlil (the main god of the Sumerians) were probably all the same entity.

However, I have done much more than spend long hours reading scholastic texts. My experience with youth groups was quite edifying. During many of the retreats I attended with young people, I saw lives transformed. I actually contributed to having young people go forward to receive Christ during a final night altar call. I spent long nights into the wee hours of the morning dialoguing with young people about why they should make God and Jesus the center of their lives. I firmly believed – at that time – that this was my holy mission. I considered it a calling from the Lord Himself. In solitude, I prayed for errant young souls. I was fully confident that the answer to their problems lay in putting God or Jesus first in their lives.

I still tremble in a good way as I remember ninety young voices singing some rousing hymn or a quiet folk tune such as "Blowing in the Wind." I was a believer then. I was convinced that I could serve God best by helping the young people I loved become better believers – or first time believers. Something deep in me stirred as I saw lives transformed and "souls on fire" for the Lord.

While I am no longer one, I spent more than half of my life as a fervent believer. I spent two years in seminary preparing to preach the gospel. I have read the archaeological, philosophical, and anthropological research of the past twenty years. After much research and increasing anguish in my soul, I have come to the conclusion that we have not been told the truth about our religious origins. We have selected the comfortable and edifying, and ignored the terrible and horrifying. What's worse is that we have ignored the evidence of archaeological discoveries. Moreover, we have ignored the resultant writings they produced. By this selective unawareness, we prevent ourselves from being able to answer some very important questions:

What was the real reason for the creation of religion?

Were the creators of our religion divine?

Did the creators of our religions really care about us?

While I will answer the above three questions briefly, a much more thorough discussion of these questions lies in *Past Shock: The Origin of Religion and Its Impact upon the Human Soul.* I intend in this material to discuss and answer three other equally important questions:

Is religion harmful to the human soul?

Is an even greater form of religion possible?

Is there one true religion?

A BRIEF HISTORY OF RELIGION

Twelve thousand years ago, a group of very advanced beings created humans as a worker race. Until then, the "gods" were working in the mines and on the point of mutiny. The ruling force decided that interfering with the evolution of beings on this planet was a better idea than having a breakdown in discipline. Thus, they created humanity as a worker force. This was a genetic cross between *homo erectus* and themselves. We did not turn out like they had planned. We were too intelligent, curious, and rebellious. We especially hated doing menial work. The genetic experimentation continued. However, a form of conditioning was added, which would insure that we would work without complaint, fight their wars, and provide them adulation as gods. This conditioning led to our first experience of organized religion.

Thus, religion was a tool to keep the newly created humans obedient and rigorously disciplined to accomplish the aims of those who created the religions.

Were the creators of religion divine? No. They simply told us they were divine, and we were not yet advanced enough to see through their lies. The newly created humans were willing to work hard for what they thought were divine beings. Technologically advanced does, in no way, mean spiritually advanced.

Did the creators of our religions really care about us? That depends on your viewpoint. They saw us as valuable to the degree that we were able to relieve them of work they didn't want to do. They saw us as valuable when we would fight wars for them. And they must have seen us as entertaining when we worshipped them or played games for them. (The Greek Olympics were originally created as an entertainment for the gods on Mount Olympus.)

A common thread that runs through all the answers to these three questions is that religion was created to manipulate and motivate us. The focus was not on our spiritual growth as much as it was getting us to do what the "gods" wanted.

IS RELIGION HARMFUL TO THE HUMAN SOUL?

Yes, much more than we are willing to admit to ourselves. The main harm that religion does is substitute belief for spiritual experience. Beliefs can be manipulated much more easily than actual experience. This is not to say that religion is against spiritual experience; however, the focus of most religions is getting its followers to believe certain tenets of the religion. What is most ironic about this is that the founders of most of the great world religions were nowhere near as concerned about belief as their eventual followers.

Jesus, Mohammed, and Buddha would probably be shocked to see what was happening with the religions they are said to have founded. Jesus would probably wince in horror seeing that some young girl was missing a dance because her religion deemed it sinful. Mohammed would most likely cringe in disbelief if he saw all the jihad's (holy wars) that have been spawned in his name. Buddha probably would have no interest in all the pomp and circumstance linked to the rituals done in his name. He would probably cry about the fact that young monks have to memorize 64,000 aphorisms.

In the Christian religion, many fundamental rituals are linked to the human experience. It becomes difficult to determine whether the experience is coming from a solid archetypal conditioning or whether the experience is a genuine spiritual experience. When one hears Bach's magnificent *B Minor Mass* or Handel's *Messiah*, is the person moved by God, good music... or both? Yet another question must be considered. If we are deeply moved by a great piece of religious classical music or a simple hymn tune, couldn't it be possible that we are reinforcing the negative conditioning inflicted upon us thousands of years ago?

I passionately love Handel's oratorio *Israel in Egypt*. Its choruses are stirring musical masterpieces proclaiming the victory of Jehovah and the Israelites over the forces of Pharaoh. As a young teenager, this deepened my Christian faith and further "convinced" me that Jehovah was indeed the true God. Now I realize that this wonderful music only more deeply etched my experience as a believer and blocked my growth as a soul. I now realize that the composer Handel was much greater than the Jehovah he was celebrating. No one among those pretender gods (entities who lied to us by telling us that they were God) could have written something as magnificent as *Israel in Egypt*.

They were technologically advanced far beyond what we are now. However, in matters of the soul, they were cretins. Not one of them could have written a Wordsworth sonnet. None of them could have sculpted Michelangelo's *David*. (The great sculptures of the world were all done by humans honoring the gods.) No pretender god could have even come close to composing something as magnificent as Beethoven's *Ninth Symphony*.

Beethoven has brought us more closely aligned with joy than any of the pretender gods did with their created religions. In one of the greatest incidents of cosmic irony, a group of "gods" actually created something greater than themselves: *homo sapiens*. Whatever Beethoven was tapping into was something higher than Jehovah – Beethoven was most likely tapping into the true God, what theologian Paul Tillich referred to as "the God beyond God." And this brings us to a question much more important than if religion is harmful to the soul. Another question should be considered:

Is religion blocking us from experiencing the true God?

That question will be discussed in more detail later.

IS A GREATER FORM OF RELIGION POSSIBLE?

The answer to this is a firm yes. However, I immediately pose another question:

Is a good form of religion possible?

The main question above, before this one, actually begged the question. A better form of religion is definitely possible; however, is it a good idea? If religion is a reinforcement of conditioning, it is not a good idea. If religion is something that frees the human race to experience the true God, then – despite how rare this might be – it is a good idea. Malcolm Muggeridge in *Jesus Rediscovered,* claimed that the closer a person came to God, the more alienated he felt from his religion. He or she is coming closer to God – the true God. This has a habit of doing that to people despite the wailing consternations of religious leaders. The problem with organized religion is that it is like a TV dinner: what's inside the box is never as good as the picture on the box. Organized religion promises God and delivers conditioning to belief-structures. It's a losing proposition – no matter how good it makes some people feel.

Finding the true God can happen much more easily outside of structured religion. The problem is that people have become addicted to ritual and conditioned belief. This provides deeper conditioning and causes both guilt and withdrawal pains. Add to this some religious strictures that will deem your withdrawal – and even your liberation – as "falling away" and thus sinful, and the experience of the "God beyond God" becomes even more difficult.

Just as the ancient religions had priests to tell people what to think and what "God hath ordained," we Americans have ministers, priests, and rabbis. Ninety percent of such people I have met – and I have met hundreds – are very good people. Unlike the ancient creators of our religions, many do not want to harm you or manipulate you. However, they do want to tell you what to believe, and in this they are unwittingly doing spiritual harm. Many times I was positively influenced by a youth minister who helped me by caring about me as a person, yet harmed me by keeping me locked into a rigid belief system that too often blocked spiritual experience. I was so beguiled by the goodness of the person that I was incapable of exploring whether the system had value.

So where does a young person get his morality? This is a good question and a very tough answer. The religion of Taoism claims that morality pushed to excess creates immorality (*Tao Te Ching*). Buddhism explores a middle path between the extremes of life codes. Christianity is much more rigid (despite the Christian liberty explained in *Romans 14*). And this very rigidity blocks the direct experience of God.

With the way that many spiritual leaders and gurus of the world's great religions act, one would swear that there was no God available for help. Many in the Islamic faith feel that they have to fight holy wars in order to be true to their faith. They give lip service to Allah. They act as if they have to get it done themselves. Christians are not free of this mentality. While they claim the power of the Holy Spirit, many act as if the Holy Spirit has no power at all. They spend serious money for lighting and sound systems to insure that the experience is magnificent – even if it isn't Godly.

Those who experience God directly do not have the need of a belief system. In fact, after such an experience, any belief system is considered irrelevant. The Holy Spirit is not locked into such a sorority mentality that he/she/it will perform only for members of the fold. All the great religious texts reveal that this isn't the case. God – the "God beyond God" – is available for all. The great tragedy is that most religious people simply aren't interested. Their interest lies mainly in a God who fits comfortably into their limited paradigm. If they experienced the true God, those paradigms would shatter, and that can be a very frightening experience for many. Meanwhile, the "God" of organized religion continues to be a warrior demanding a battle for the faith, demanding the embracing of an ancient belief system, which was as false then as it is now.

IS THERE ONE TRUE RELIGION?

No! A thousand times no! This is one of the most soul-depleting beliefs ever inflicted upon humanity. While this is not worthy of the true God, it is typical of religions founded in the name of the ancient beings who claimed to be God. Only pretenders to divinity could inflict such a demand on an "inferior" species (ancient humans).

The true God is neither petty nor insecure. However, one who pretends is always insecure in the reality that he might be found out. The true God does not fear being found out; he probably would like just to be found. Standing between the human experience and the true God lies a mighty conditioning so powerful that finding this true God is not likely. Humans, after thousands of years of ancient conditioning, find themselves more comfortable continuing this conditioning than they do looking for the truth. What is conditioning is comfortable and predictable. Unfortunately, it is not true.

What ironically blocks our experiencing the true God is our obsession to be a part of the true religion. Like the college student who wants to be in the best fraternity, so do humans want to feel the exclusivity of belonging to the true religion. True, Roman Catholics no longer burn people at the stake for heretical beliefs. Many Protestant sects – like the Catholics – believe that if people live a good life according to their faith, they will find eternal rest. Yet, at other extremes, the many facets of the fundamentalist Christian experience continue to warn about dancing, dream analysis, meditation, and the large umbrella of the New Age movement. It is not a matter of whether organized religion has sane and insane levels; it is, however, more about the pathetically few adherents of any religion who are willing to look at what happened thousands of years ago that insanely continue to live on in modern religion.

No, there is no true religion. Frankly, I doubt very much if different religions have fragments of the truth. That New Age morsel is more a truism than a reality – words thrown out to get nods of agreement rather than inspire a search for the experience of God.

This is not fertile ground for the Holy Spirit to operate. Because God is a creator on the spiritual level, He (She, It) logically would want his creations to be co-creators with Him (Her, It). A God who creates souls, various dimensions of reality, and perhaps even the Universe would not want His subjects going through endless rituals and incessantly praising His name. He would not elect – to the exclusion of others – a small tribe in Asia or a group of only one color in Africa. And He certainly would not determine that there was only one religion by which any seeker could embrace Him. He would never sink to asserting that Beta Pi's are in, but Kappa Sigmas are going to burn. He would not experience anger if a Sigma Chi married one of the forbidden Chi Omegas. The true God – Tillich's "God beyond God" – does not involve Himself in such silly stuff.

That silly stuff persists because we voluntarily continue to brainwash ourselves with lies that we swear to God are true. Never should we blame ourselves for this, because we were highly conditioned to believe that we have never been conditioned. These beliefs were etched into us in great terror and they remain at the cellular level. We were spiritually raped by pretenders. Thousands of years later, we are still worshipping those who raped us.

This is the greatest harm of religion. We voluntarily keep ourselves in hell when the kingdom of heaven lies deep within us. Religion does great harm when it continues the conditioning of the belief that what happens to us after we die is more important than what happens to us now. However, one of the greatest harms of religion is that it keeps alive a woeful conditioning that aids people in feeling good when they continue their slave ways. Yet it also causes eruptions of guilt just at the point when one begins walking on the path to spiritual liberation. The harm of religion is that it has kept people worshipping their chains and praising the entities who chained their souls.

What is the harm of religion? It hinders the experience of God.

If God is saying, "Embrace me: I can take you to higher levels," many will reply, "No thanks. I'm comfortable with what I got. It may not give me power, but it sure does give me certainty."

Once again, God says, "I am deep within you. Embrace me there." The reply is often, "Get thee behind me, Satan. I don't listen to that New Age nonsense."

One more time God says, "I want to set you free," and the reply is, "Sorry, in my religion, the only way you can truly be free is to be a slave to God."

These souls are riding round and round on a merry-go-round reaching for the brass ring. Every once in a while someone catches one of the brass rings and edifies the masses with rousing testimony. This inspires more to get on the merry-go-round and even more fervently lunge for the brass ring. Round and round they go – chanting, singing, shouting slogans, and making a "joyful" noise. What none of them understands is that going for the brass ring is not the name of the game. The name of game is getting off the merry-go-round.

Chapter Five

Questions and Answers on:
"Is Religion Harmful?"

Don't you think it would be cruel to take a person's religion away from them? Some people have spent their whole lives nurturing a belief system.

I agree with you. I would never – even if I had the power – take away a person's belief system. Some people get great pleasure in rattling people's cages concerning their religion.

But aren't you rattling people's cages in what you are saying here?

You came to a lecture entitled "Is Religion Harmful?" You're an adult and I assume you have good powers of discernment. If you were looking for religious rhetoric, you certainly were aware that this would not be the place to find it.

How do we stop the harm that religion is doing? Do you have any suggestions?

I'm not even sure that it's a good idea to attempt to do this. Many good books are written on the subject, and this movement has been going on for some time. A century ago a man named Robert Ingersoll was packing the houses lecturing on this same theme. However, he was probably a man long before his time. He did not have the benefit of the ancient writings and archeological evidence that we have now.

So you think we're going to experience a revival – or perhaps even a de-revival?

Now there's an interesting concept. Rather than a de-revival, I think we are closer to seeing a flower that is going to bloom. The Protestant Reformation didn't really begin with Martin Luther in Germany. It started in the late 1300's with John Hus and Jerome of Prague – and a military leader named general John Zitzka. All they wanted was to be able to read the Bible in Czech – their own language. Each of these men died for this cause – along with many other brave souls. The consensus reality was that this attempt at reformation was short-lived and futile. Yet Martin Luther himself said, "This Reformation was bought by the blood of John (Hus) and Jerome." They sowed seeds that grew 130 years later in Germany.

I believe that the seeds Robert Ingersoll – and others like him – sowed a century ago are beginning to sprout.

Isn't organized religion stronger than ever? Cults are on the rise. The Christian Right is gaining great power.

I know that this is going to sound naïve, but some wonderful things are starting to happen – things that are happening on their own. Jordan Maxwell – a very good friend of mine – could barely muster an audience when he first started talking about ancient religious conspiracies. Now he fills entire lecture halls. People's hunger for an alternative view is increasing exponentially.

He is one of the writers of a book called *The Book the Church Doesn't Want You to Read*. This is an excellent book by writers like Alan Snow, Jordan Maxwell, and Steve Allen – more than forty writers (including Robert Ingersoll) who want to inform you about what you have not been told regarding our religious past and our religious present.

Tim Leedam, the editor of *The Book Your Church Doesn't Want You to Read*, claims that he went to lecture to a group of Protestant ministers and was experiencing fear and trepidation. He knew these were good people and that he wasn't going to be lynched, but he was concerned that his material would turn them off.

Not so. They were angry – but neither at Tim nor his book. They were angry that they had never been told about any of this during their theological education.

What is it in our supposedly lurid past that could rattle and shake up a group of ministers?

Do you have a spare three days?

Seriously, this is a very deep issue – and quite frankly not very pleasant. I have material here that covers some of that issue. Right now, I am working on another book which attempts to explain what happened thousands of years ago that raped our very concept of God and the divine.

Succinctly put – if anyone *can* put this material succinctly – what happened thousands of years ago was not pretty. Jehovah, who claimed that he created the heavens and the earth, was not a very nice entity. He wasn't anything close to being God. Instead, he was a mentally deranged warlord who told the Israelites that he was God and that he had chosen them for a special mission.

Some mission! This involved marching around the hot desert while many starved to death. When people complained that they were hungry, Jehovah responded with poisonous snakes, beatings, and death sentences. He demanded that a man be stoned to death because he was picking up sticks on the Sabbath. He told his "chosen people" that they would have to eat their own excrement if they didn't do as they were told. This was not a compassionate, all-loving God. This was a psychologically deranged warlord.

I've heard you lecture before and you have claimed that you should look for the good in even the worst people. Could you possibly say anything good about Jehovah?

I'm sorry…I'm laughing. Shoot, this is a real stretch. Yeah, I remember something from my seminary days. Jehovah had come to one of the minor prophets and claimed that he was going to destroy Israel. He came back a couple of days later and said, "I cannot destroy Israel."

Before any of you start weeping from being so moved, I must tell you that many Bible scholars feel that there were actually four Jehovahs. They have figured this out by studying the linguistic structures of what the Jehovahs spoke. Jehovah – or Yahweh as the scholars like to call him – was an epithet. Not an epithet like "damn" or "hell," but an unspeakable given name – called a Tetragrammaton. The fourth Jehovah was probably only neurotic. He actually showed some compassion.

But what about people like me who believe that Jehovah is indeed God?

I am truly sorry that you believe that, but I can't judge you – because I believed that same thing for a period of time probably longer than you have been alive. I firmly believe that this is a counterproductive belief. However, I believed that because of my conditioning. As a very young boy, I read the Bible on my own. I remember the crisis I had when I read the story about a group of Israelites carrying the Ark of the Covenant. As it was about to tip over, Uzzah – one of the Israelites – ran up and attempted to keep it from tipping over. According to the biblical account, Uzzah was struck dead by Jehovah.

I could not even then understand how a loving God would strike dead a man who was trying to help him. So I discussed this with my parents, and they said that some things about God we just can't understand. I then asked my minister, and he said that God had given very strict orders that no one touch the Ark of the Covenant. He went on to say that God's rules had to be followed. He topped it off with the old saw that God in his infinite wisdom knew what he was doing.

Then, I went to see the movie *David and Bathsheba*. Now I got to watch Uzzah struck dead by the wrath of God. But to complicate things further, the movie ends with Gregory Peck as David intentionally touching the Ark and not being struck dead. So now we have David, a flagrant adulterer, not being struck dead and Uzzah, someone who was trying to help, being zapped by an angry Jehovah.

I had to go back to the Bible to find that David didn't really touch the Ark. However, at that tender young age, there was no one to tell me that this was not God but instead "gods" who had no spiritual value at all. No one was around to tell me that Uzzah was probably electrocuted – as would anyone have been if he had touched the Ark.

This is a roundabout way of answering the question, but it points out that I was conditioned from a very young age to believe that Jehovah was God. I was conditioned by very well-meaning parents who themselves had been conditioned at a very young age, as were their parents. We believe that Jehovah was God because of conditioning that has been going on for thousands of years. However, once one begins examining it, one finds the evidence for Jehovah being God just doesn't hold up. We are so well-programmed that we feel guilty if we feel anything different. However, feeling something different is the only way to go. Jehovah is not God – he never was.

Do you think I get joy out of saying that? My mouth goes dry every time I make a statement like that. I feel like a dog who's crapping on the rug.

I remember coming home one day and being shocked that my dog Sappho didn't run up to greet me. I knew there was no way my wife could have gotten home first, so this appeared very strange. Then I saw it: Sappho had taken a very big dump on the rug. Like angry

Jehovah, I called out to Sappho with a deep, resonant voice – you know, like Jehovah did after Adam and Eve did their no-no. I knew Sappho was in the house. After fifteen minutes of searching, I found a trembling Sappho underneath some clothes in the closet. At that moment I realized that I had forgotten to let Sappho out to attend to nature. Yet I was still looking at a guilt-ridden dog who had done nothing wrong.

I hugged her, stroked her, and probably over-dosed her with Milk Bones, and she still felt guilt. The difference between me and Jehovah is that Jehovah would have just whomped her and screamed "Bad dog!" I feel that whoever we worship as God should be much more compassionate than Jehovah – and certainly more compassionate than I am.

If the true God is so compassionate, why didn't He intervene when Jehovah was doing all these nasty things?

Well, Joe, God in His infinite wisdom knew what he was...

No, seriously, I honestly don't know the answer to that one. If I had the power of Jehovah and his ilk, I would have tried to stop it. We do have accounts of people who did try to make a difference. In the *Atra Hasis* – a Sumerian epic that predates the Bible and is the established foundation for at least the first six chapters of Genesis, Enki (the brother of Enlil) knows that a flood is coming. Enlil – whom many historians believe was Jehovah – wants all of the human race to conveniently drown. However, Enki warns Utnatpishtim that a flood is coming and instructs him on how to build an ark. Utnatpishtim – damn, that's a rough one to pronounce. No wonder they changed his name to Noah. Anyhow, Enki warns what's-his-face, so that some of humanity can be saved.

This is where it gets very interesting. According to the *Atra Hasis*, all of the Annunaki (the gods) are hovering above watching millions of humans frantically drowning. Many of them begin weeping.

Finally, Jehovah/Enlil begins weeping. At that point brother Enki says, "Guess what I did?"

You would think that Enlil would have been possessed with joy hearing that some humans had been saved. However, he went into a violent rage and wouldn't talk to Enki for weeks. The point here is that some of the gods did care – they did want to help, despite the fact that they were exploiting us.

William Bramley, in his groundbreaking book *The Gods of Eden,* tells of a group called "The Brotherhood of the Serpent" who were concerned about the spiritual development of this newly formed human race. They secretly gave spiritual instruction to the humans and told them flat out that the gods were not God. From this position, you can get a better perspective of the Garden of Eden incident, and Prometheus' decision to steal fire from the gods and give it to humanity. This Brotherhood of the Serpent was not the devil or anything evil; this was a group of "gods" who were sick and tired of the harm that the actions of the other "gods" were doing to people. That harm is still going on today. However, this time we don't have any outlaw gods to help us. We're on our own.

I have problems with your statement that we're on our own.

I do, too. That was a bad choice of words.

Long ago something happened – something so painful that few people possess the courage to look at it. Thousands of years ago, a group of beings raped our souls. That not being horrible enough, this group of "advanced" beings claimed that this soul rape was good for us – that it was being done for our own good. These beings who raped our souls not only violated our spiritual sovereignty, but also totally twisted the way we would view God. In fact, they increased the egregiousness of their violation by daring to tell us that *they* were God.

Julian Jaynes, author of *The Origins of Consciousness and the Breakdown of the Bicameral Mind*, claimed that this period was a period of intense psychosis for the emerging human race. The entities that created this spiritual rape had no sense of honor and did not respect the sovereignty of the human race. Instead, they trained this emerging species how to fight their wars, how to work hard for their masters, and how to worship those beings as God. It was a horrible time. It was a time that created what we are experiencing today: This is past shock, shock from the past that we haven't even come close to getting over.

Chapter Six

The Ten Commandments

1. Thou shalt have no other Gods before me.

2. Thou shalt not make unto me any graven image.

3. Thou shall not take the name of the Lord thy God in vain.

4. Thou shalt remember the Sabbath day and keep it holy.

5. Thou halt honor thy mother and father.

6. Thou shalt not kill.

7. Thou shalt not commit adultery.

8. Thou shalt not steal.

9. Thou shalt not bear false witness against thy neighbor.

10. Thou shalt not covet thy neighbor's house, wife, manservant, nor maidservant.

Chapter Seven

The Ten Realizations:

Realization Number One

A Person on a Spiritual Journey will almost always Experience a Dark Night of the Soul

It is very important that we include this realization first because, as bad as it might feel, it means that you are making progress. This is the problem with mainstream organized religions: they do not see the wealth of this experience. If you are experiencing a dark night of the soul, you have a feeling of darkness. Back in the Middle Ages, Saint John of the Cross wrote about this experience. The Hindus refer to it as "the long winter." However, well-meaning people will tell you that the devil is causing this experience, or they will tell you that you are "falling away."

You are not falling away and you are not being possessed by the devil. Instead, you are moving closer to the True God. You have many years of conditioning to overcome and this is part of the purging process. I won't tell you that it doesn't hurt, because it does. Sometimes it feels downright awful. You feel empty. You feel that you are doing something wrong because it doesn't feel good. The thing is that you *can* feel good, but not by returning to the path that you were conditioned to believe was the truth.

Your previous path provided those things that released endorphins – made you feel good. You remember the sermons that made you feel uplifted. But there is something deeper moving within you – something that wants to take you to the next level. Since most people are gregarious and enjoy being accepted by "believers," they miss that acceptance.

The dark night of the soul is aptly named. It feels mighty dark and empty sometimes. But there is nothing wrong with you. If you have this feeling, it does not mean you have strayed from the path; it, in actuality, means that you are walking on the right path.

But why does it have to feel so bad, you ask. The answer is simple but not easy: you are making room in your heart and soul for a higher way of being. Many make the mistake of looking for a true religion. There is no such thing as a true religion. Organized religion is the problem, and you are now ready to leap into the abyss and experience something truly spiritual. That does not mean going from one organized religion to the other. This will temporarily make you feel good, but the good feeling will not last.

Friends, well-meaning friends, will urge you to pray harder – failing to realize that what you are experiencing may be an answer to prayer. Something or someone higher wants you free, and the dark night of the soul is the way to freedom. Most people are uniquely human; they just want to feel good and will accept anything – *anything* – that provides that good feeling. The problem is that this good feeling comes as a result of conditioning and has nothing to do with your own unique spiritual path.

This is not the time to take anti-depressants or get high. This is not a time to wish that you were dead. The irony of all this is that people who have had near-death experiences generally return and find that they can no longer relate to anything that smacks of organized religion. This is not to suggest that you run out and have a near-death experience, but if you know anyone who has had one, you might want to talk to them; they will understand what you are going through.

Now the good news. There is light at the end of the tunnel. You come out of the dark night of the soul stronger and more spiritual than you have been all your life. You emerge more spiritually free, and this is the gift of the dark night of the soul: more freedom at the soul level. You may feel like dancing and you certainly want others to have the experience, but they may not be ready. You had this experience because you were ready, and that is a badge of honor.

I had my dark night of the soul when I was in seminary. This was a Bible-believing, fundamentalist seminary. I remember a time when I had a tray of food during lunch and I went to sit down with a group of people who all happened to be in my Greek class. I started to sit down with them and they asked me to move to another table. They claimed, "We just can't handle you." This is one of the greatest of ironies because it was reading the *New Testament* in the original Greek that most likely began my dark night of the soul. Much of what I learned from that experience is written in these ten realizations.

Chapter Eight

Realization Number Two

Of all the Sacred Books and Scriptures, None of Them is the Word of God, Including the *Holy Bible*

There exist many great books that could be considered sacred books. *The Damaphada,* which is a volume of sacred scriptures and is the holy book of Buddhism, is a wonderful collection of what Buddha said after he spent six years meditating under the Bo tree. The *Tao Te Ching* is another great book which gave me hours of edification. It is the writings of Lao Tse and is meant to give greater dimension to the religion of Taoism.

However, in this section I am going to stick to the the *Holy Bible.* The *Holy Bible* is so full of contradictions that I cannot imagine God being so inconsistent. Much of the early part of the Bible consists of long and ponderous instructions on how to prepare sacrifices. The book of Joshua goes into long diatribes explaining the borders of Israel. Reading this section alone is the best cure for insomnia that I know. Moreover, the series of begats that began the *Book of Matthew* could cause one to scream, "Enough!"

However, a book's being boring and a chore to read is not enough to dismiss it from being the word of God. For this we have to go to the Council of Nicea in 325 C.E. and realize what was happening. There, men argued and put to a vote which writings would go into the Bible. How the book of *Philemon* made it into the Bible is still a mystery to me. How the *Books of Enoch* were left out is equally a mystery. Some books made it into the Bible by a score of less than twenty votes. It was like Congress: there were many lobbyists for certain books.

54

If Martin Luther had had his way, the book of *Revelation* would have been expurgated. Anything referring to reincarnation was taken out by a majority vote. The idea was that you had one lifetime to make it to eternal bliss or eternal damnation.

Scribes also had their moments, and when they felt that something was not right, they changed it – or sometimes added to it. Most theologians believe this to be the truth. Thus, "Go ye therefore into the world and teach the gospel" was probably never said by Jesus. Yet we have missionaries all over the world "preaching the Gospel."

Anyone looking at the four accounts of the resurrection can see some severe contradictions. One states that there was a mighty earthquake and that an angel appeared and rolled away the stone. Another version has one angel sitting in the lying place of Jesus. Yet another version has Peter and John going first to the tomb and then going back to fetch the two Marys (Mary, the mother of Jesus, and Mary Magdalene). In only one account does Jesus appear at the tomb. In three accounts, the stone is already rolled away; in another an angel appears and rolls away the stone.

I commend the editors of the *Holy Bible* for some of the things that they left in, though I can't understand it. Why not exorcise the time that Jehovah threw down thousands of poisonous snakes because the children of Israel were complaining about the lack of food and water? Why not exorcise the bit where Jehovah changed his mind about murdering thousands more of his people because Phineas noticed an Israelite man taking a Midianite woman into a tent and followed them in and stabbed them to death with a javelin? Jehovah was so happy, he decided to cancel the slaughter that he was engaged in. Why not exorcise the story of a group of small children who yelled out "Hey, baldy!" to the prophet Elisha and were ripped to pieces when Jehovah sent a couple of angry bears into their midst?

Anyone carefully reading the *Old Testament* would have a hard time believing that this was the father of Jesus.

Chapter Nine

Realization Number Three

Realize that it is not Necessary to go to Church, Mass, or Temples to Please the True God

Churches, Mass, and temples are brainwashing tools left over from ancient times. Much of it is for the sole purpose of reinforcing beliefs. The one time that I went to church with some of my Catholic friends, I did not kneel before the statue of Mary as I went into the pew. This offended some of my friends. What I had gone against was a belief structure that they had been self-instilling for years, and I had dared to breach it.

I had my own personal "dark night of the soul" when I would say the Apostle's Creed. I would say to myself: "There's nothing here I really believe anymore." Yet I would go to church with my father because it pleased him. He already knew I was an agnostic, but he had his hopes that I would "return to the fold." Singing hymns and reciting creeds is a spiritual reinforcement of ideas, and may keep people on the path of belief rather than the path of experience.

We went to chapel every day when I was in seminary. I enjoyed singing the hymns, but I also realized that this was as much a brainwashing tool as the recitation of beliefs. As I move further on my own spiritual path, I realize that I have some real problems with "Onward Christian Soldiers." I now realize that my past upbringing was responsible for the goose bumps I got when I sang, "Onward Christian soldiers, marching as to war." I have the same problem when singing "Amazing Grace" and the expression "that saved a wretch like me." I consider the subconscious harm this does when people refer to themselves as "wretches" who need to be saved. Yet when 150 bagpipes play it at the Edinburgh Black Watch without the words, I become genuinely moved. It's a great tune.

You might claim that people just say the words without thinking about them, or when the Mass was in Latin, people didn't understand it anyway. But even in Latin, the conditioning is there. Going to a mass, church service, or temple can only deepen that conditioning and keep you locked in a state of belief – and a state of belief actually hinders your experience of the True God. (Whether you believe or don't believe in a True God doesn't really matter.)

I was part of the Methodist Youth Fellowship because I wanted to be there with friends. I firmly believe that most people go to church and allow themselves to go through that unconscious conditioning because they want to see their friends. They just go through the motions. This is certainly not true of most fundamentalist churches where the people come to reinforce their beliefs. They don't want Satan to take control of their lives and this weekly surge arms them with "the power of the Lord."

I am amazed that anyone could believe that God would actually send a group of people, or even one person, to experience eternal torment. Yet the fundamentalist Christians believe that unsaved people will endure such suffering. I am amazed that Roman Catholics believe in an eternal hell. The amazement continues with the belief in Purgatory, a place where you can be "purged" of your sins until your soul is clean enough to enter heaven. I cringed in horror as Pope Benedict claimed that hell was a place of flames, and that one does indeed burn for eternity. I cringe when I think of Israel pushing Palestinians off their land because of something that was stated more than two thousand years ago.

Yet this is what happens when people go once a week to reinforce their belief systems. When you free yourself from the bonds of the evangelical, you don't have to take it upon yourself to win souls away from their weekly worship. You'll have enough people praying that you "return to the fold" and worry that you are putting your soul into mortal danger.

I will wrap up with a story from my college teaching career. Eric was a young boy that I had an amazing rapport with. He said to me one day as we were walking in the parking lot, "Mr. Barranger, it really bothers me that you won't be in heaven with me." I put my hand on his shoulder and said, "Think of it, Eric, you'll be spending eternity with nothing but born again Christians." His face went as white as a sheet of paper, and he couldn't say anything. The issue never came up again.

Chapter Ten
Realization Number Four

Jehovah was not God, and He still Isn't

The Old Testament Jehovah was not God, although he sure took great pains to convince the Israelites that he was. Instead, he was a cruel warlord who must have been highly advanced technologically. He was also a mass murderer who killed for the pure joy of it. In *Leviticus 19*, he says, "I am the Lord" fifteen times. One gets the sense that he was trying to convince himself as well as the Israelites. He also made promises and broke them. He was cruel to the point where he even killed his own "chosen people" when he was in the desert with the Israelites. He was the Adolph Hitler of the *Old Testament* – although Hitler murdered less people and did not include his own.

It is sad that people still worship Jehovah today. If he was indeed God, he would have been more loving and compassionate; but instead he ruled with fear and loathing. He hated the fact that the Canaanites were worshipping Baal, and that must have been the reason that he made the first of the Ten Commandments: "Thou shall have no other Gods before me." He could not have made much of an impression, because as soon as Moses went off to the mountain to be with Jehovah, the Israelites *en masse* melted down their gold and fashioned a calf to worship instead.

Jehovah was most likely the Sumerian god Enlil, who hated humans. He complained that they made so much noise that they deprived him of sleep. According to Bramley, his brother Enki formed a group called "The Brotherhood of the Snake," which saw the spiritual potential in the newly created humans. Enki was probably the one who urged Noah to build the Ark so that a portion of the human race could be saved. Both Enki and Enlil (Jehovah) knew that a flood was coming and that it would wipe out the human race. When Enki told Enlil that he had saved some of the humans, Enlil went into a rage. Enki was most likely the Serpent in the Garden of Eden.

According to *Genesis 3*, Jehovah went into a rage when he found that Adam and Eve had eaten of the fruit of the forbidden tree. Yet Jehovah was a liar, claiming that even if they touched the tree, they would "surely die." The serpent was telling the truth – that their eyes would be opened and they would be as gods. Jehovah would have none of that and did his best to scare Adam and Eve away from the tree – which, by the way, was in the middle of the garden. Jehovah did not want the humans to become anything like gods – he was determined that they remain more like cosmic pets and do menial work and worship him as the True God.

How anyone can read the *Old Testament* and think that Jehovah was God is beyond me. When the Israelites complained that they were both hungry and thirsty, he resorted to his "godly" motivation. He brought down thousands of poisonous snakes. These snakes bit the people and thousands died. Only Moses was able to convince Jehovah that this was not only excessive, but was also killing potential warriors. So Jehovah did something that scientists have not been able to figure out to this day. He had the people fashion a brass snake and put it on top of a pole. He promised that anyone who looked at the snake would be cured. Thus, people looked at the brass snake and did not die. This, of course, happened only after thousands of people already had.

In one of Jehovah's lowest moments, he was told that a man was picking up sticks on the Sabbath. "God" instantly came up with a punishment: the man was stoned to death for breaking one of the Ten Commandments: thou shall remember the Sabbath and keep it holy. Evidently, picking up a stick was not holy, and the poor guy "deserved" to die.

Jehovah fashioned the Ten Commandments and figured they were more for the people than they were for him. What about leading by example? Forget it! He stole, killed, and even ordered someone to be murdered on the Sabbath. When Joshua finally made it to Jericho, he was instructed that nothing should be left breathing. He did save the life of a prostitute named Rahab, who hid the spies who came into Jericho. In payment for this favor, she extracted a promise from them that when the Israelites invaded Jericho and slaughtered everything breathing, they would spare her family. This was another of Jehovah's *quid pro quos*: you please me and I won't hack you to death.

Jehovah loved the shedding of blood. When Pharaoh agreed to release the Israelite slaves, Jehovah claimed that he would harden his heart so that he would change his mind. When Joshua made an agreement to make peace with a tribe called the Hivites, Jehovah not only hardened the heart of the king, but also hardened the hearts of the whole Hivite tribe so they would attack Joshua and force him into battle, that the might and glory of Jehovah would be demonstrated.

Is this a god? Yes, just like Baal was a god, and Zeus was a god. Was Jehovah *the* God? No! He didn't even come close.

Chapter Eleven
Realization Number Five

Guilt has No Place in the Religious Experience

I am going to get a little personal here. For much of my life, I was probably the all-time champion of guilt. Thanks to my conditioning, I could slip into guilt with the smallest of stimuli. Guilt did not make me a better person. In fact, it set me up for depression and anger.

After I had been "saved," I walked through the halls of my high school and would see the cheerleaders walking in their short skirts. I would slip into the wildest of fantasies. Eventually, I began to feel extreme guilt because this was not part of the evangelical paradigm. I would pray to be released from Satan's grip. Then another cheerleader walked by, and it appeared that Satan was winning. I had no idea that this was just raging hormones. This had nothing to do with Satan or, for that matter, God.

However, it was in seminary that I felt the greatest guilt. I did not have that programmed certainty that most of my fellow seminarians at least appeared to have. In fact, when I raised my hand to ask a question, I would hear groans from others in the class, and that alone caused me guilt. One time, the professor was assuring us that God never changed his mind. I raised my hand, endured the groans, and mentioned there was indeed a time when God changed his mind. Isaiah had been told by Jehovah that he was going to take the life of one of his friends. Isaiah pleaded with Jehovah that he not be killed that night. Jehovah finally told Isaiah that he would let the man live another fifteen years. I mentioned that this was an example of God changing his mind. The Professor said, "God did not change his mind; He repented his decision." I then said, "That's a bunch of semantic crap." I was sitting in the back and I could see many faces turning around and looking at me with anger. I felt guilt big-time then.

My guilt was inappropriate. I had a genuine comment to make and it received an inadequate response. In fact, guilt is rarely ever an appropriate response. When growing up, I would hear my mother say, "Aren't you ashamed of yourself?" She would keep saying it until I slipped myself into a genuine guilt mode and felt terrible. Guilt is a programmed reaction to something you have done or are thinking about. It usually has something to do with the past. In relation to human behavior, it has no value at all. If you do something that you are "guilty" of, regret is a more appropriate response.

It causes pain and it rarely changes human behavior. In fact, Wayne Dyer claims that it often insures that you will do the same act or have the same thought again. Wayne's first book, *Your Erroneous Zones*, deals very effectively with guilt and worry, and I recommend it highly.

Think how willingly we cause dogs to feel guilty. Fido leaves a mess on the rug, and most people respond with anger. Some even use the ASPCA approved method of folding a newspaper and swatting the dog. The dog at this time has no guilt. It is merely fulfilling a function of nature. However, it eventually (and hopefully) becomes housebroken when it receives enough disapproval, anger, and pain. We have to program the dog to feel guilty; otherwise the rugs will smell and the dog will believe that it can defecate wherever it wants. Although a dog is not born with the stain of sin that Adam and Eve allegedly committed, he also has to be swatted a lot.

I am convinced that Jehovah invented sin and the guilt that goes along with it. It is ludicrous to think that we are born "guilty" because of what Adam and Eve did. In fact, what they did eventually liberated humanity. Being tossed out of the Garden of Eden was probably the best thing that happened to the human race. We were on our own and were forced to grow. The worst thing that happened to the human race was the forty years spent in the desert. There, we learned how to be warriors and kill in the name of God. In fact, many of the wars that have been fought probably resulted from the conditioning that happened in the desert.

Think of the ease with which America invaded Iraq. Despite the fact that a majority of the American people did not want to invade Iraq, we still went – and eased our guilt by claiming that we were using "smart bombs." Not one of the "smart bombs" hit its intended target. Yet this never made the news. We even invent terms to ease our guilt. Although these bombs did in fact kill a lot of innocent people, we were made to feel less guilty because the news never said, "Innocent people were killed, and we are trying to minimize that." We said instead, "We are trying to minimize collateral damage."

In college, I felt guilty if I didn't study hard enough. The guilt made me feel so bad that it got in the way of my studying. To make a long story short, I flunked out of college at the end of my sophomore year. Yet, guilt still reigned supreme, and I went to summer school and raised my average. I didn't feel guilty when I was in summer school, but I was bored to tears because this was taking away my summer. Then, something significant happened. I was reading *Hamlet* late into the night, and I said to myself, "This is really great stuff." At one in the morning, I began the play again and stayed up until five in the morning. I was a changed person and started reading Elizabethan plays that were not part of the assignments.

This is what I hope will happen to you. This book is written with the intention of getting you to recognize experiences like I had that night. They are called epiphanies. An epiphany can be a life-changing (or at least a paradigm shifting) experience. May you have many of them.

Chapter Twelve

Realization Number Six

You Were not Born a Sinner and Most Likely Never Committed a Sin

This is quite likely dangerous territory to explore, and I seriously considered not including it in this book. But the notion that we are all born sinners because of the "Fall of Man" is an absurd idea. A loving God would not even consider such an idea. In fact, *A Course in Miracles* claims that, in God's eyes, we never sinned at all. *A Course in Miracles* was claimed to have been dictated or channeled by Jesus to correct some of the things stated in the Bible.

The fact is that God sees us as pure beings who have never sinned. There is no purgatory to purge us of our sins, and *A Course in Miracles* claims that we will not go to hell – because we are already there. The claim is that earth is hell and we make a heaven or hell with our own minds. As I mentioned before, the way out of hell is to forgive everyone who you think "sinned." The point is to see good in everyone. The spark of God is in everyone, and if that is the case, then your seeing that spark affects both you and the other person.

When I was teaching college in the 1990's, I had a student one might refer to as a died-in-the-wool punker. At times she would come into class with purple hair and the punker-type garb. Yet, she was one of my favorite students. She spoke her mind and was a true individual. I was heartbroken when she told me that she had cancer. She also hated her mother and complained incessantly about her. As we were walking across the campus one day, I said something to her that I had never said because of my own fear. I said, "Dawn, if you don't find a way to forgive and love your mother, you're going to die." I immediately thought to myself, "What an ass you are; how can you dare say a thing like that?" But I was following the leanings of my heart and it overrode the leanings of my "rational" mind. About three weeks later I saw her on campus and she stopped me and said, "You know, Barranger, I don't hate my mom anymore. In fact, I love the bitch." Dawn is still alive and I doubt very much that she still refers to her mother as a bitch.

The True God is not capable of seeing sin. Jehovah did, but he wasn't God. When Jesus said to the woman at the well, "Go and sin no more," he was not referring to a black mark on her soul, but instead was insinuating that by being an adulteress she was falling short of the target.

That is exactly what the word "sin" means in the Greek. The word is "hamartia," and it refers to an archer falling short of the target. When Paul in the *Epistle to the Romans* said, "All have sinned and come short of the glory of God," he was speaking to the people of his time. This was written by a man. The thinking of most organized religions is that we are all sinners and need to be saved. Actually, you are already saved because God sees you as a sinless person whose soul is still pure. You don't have any black marks on your soul because you went to a dance. You don't have a black mark on your soul because you thought an impure thought. And you don't have a black mark on your soul if you doubt that there is a God. If there is a God, He, She or It can handle it.

A belief in reincarnation is a sin in some circles, but let's say that you believe that you beat me to death in a previous life. I have two words for you: "Forget it." I have no desire for you to suffer because of something you might have done in a previous life. When respected Harvard professor and UFO researcher John Mack was killed by a drunk driver in England, his parents wrote to the judge trying the case and asked that he be lenient with the driver. They did not want to see him severely punished. I saw on television a woman forgive a twenty-year-old boy who had killed her eighteen-year-old daughter while driving drunk. She even asked the boy, "Can you forgive yourself?"

and he choked out, "I'm working on it."

Both the woman who lost her daughter and the parents of John Mack understood the power of forgiveness. They were closer to the True God, who simply refuses to see sin. That God sees you as a pure being, and it is only in your mind that you see yourself as a bad person or – "heaven forbid" – a sinner. This one might be a hard one to swallow. Certainly people may have hurt you deeply, or one of your parents may have walked out on you. But if you can see these people as just people in pain, then you will understand that this is the way they chose to deal with their pain. It may not seem to you to have been a *good* choice, but it was the only one they could find.

The more that you see yourself as pure, the more pure you will become at the level of your highly conditioned mind. You were not born in sin and there's a very good chance that, in God's eyes, you never have sinned.

Chapter Thirteen

Realization Number Seven

There Exists No Such Thing as a True Religion or a True Church

The problem with all religions, churches, and faiths is that they are formed by human beings. Most of the people whom religions honor had no intention of starting a church in the first place. For example, it was not Jesus but Paul who founded Christianity. And it was Charlemagne who founded the Roman Catholic Church, which many people believe is the one true religion. However, Charlemagne was not only a former pagan, he was also a politician. He realized that he must make some concessions to the pagans to make his reign flow smoothly. Thus, he chose Christianity as the official state religion because he knew that Christian principles made it easier to control people. So he took material from his former pagan religion and forged it into what we now know as the Roman Catholic Church.

Consider this: Jesus was not born on December 25th. Mithra, an earlier Persian messiah, was born then. Mithra was also referred to as *The Lamb of God*. Mithra is reported to have been crucified and resurrected three days later. Virishna, another pagan deity, was not only crucified and resurrected from the dead, but was crucified between two thieves. So when it comes to the Roman Catholic Church, and most other denominations, the very fact of historical compromise taints their truthfulness.

The concepts of purgatory and limbo are nowhere in the Bible. They were incorporated as beliefs by a vote of bishops during the many councils that were held.

Protestant evangelicals did not come up with the idea of an "altar call" to accept Jesus as one's personal savior until the Nineteenth Century. Then began the fundamentalist movement where, if you do not go through the act of receiving Jesus as your personal savior, you get to rot in hell for eternity. This concept is absurd. It postulates that we were all born into sin and that Jesus died on the cross to save us from it. People are told that all they have to do to get to heaven for eternity is say a little prayer, asking Jesus to be their personal savior.

This concept cries out for deeper thought. First of all, the reality of heaven and hell cannot be proven. In addition to which, the idea of resting for eternity sounds like a crashing bore. The evangelical concept of accepting Jesus as your personal savior (or else!) sounds more like a fire insurance policy than an act of salvation. Nevertheless, Pope Benedict recently assured us in a public proclamation that hell does in fact exist and those who go there will suffer the torment of eternal flames.

I really miss John Paul II.

The Latter-Day Saints are so convinced theirs is the True Church that every Mormon has to do missionary work before they reach a certain age. Yet their religion was not founded until the Nineteenth Century. Apparently, if Mormonism is the true religion, God sure took his own sweet time getting it right. Mormonism is based on the translation of some scrolls allegedly given to Joseph Smith by an angel who called himself Moroni. So far, only one third of these scrolls have been translated. The majority of the material is to be translated in the future. Evangelical Protestants are convinced that these scrolls are the work of the devil and they must do their best to convert Mormons to the "true faith." Jehovah's Witnesses were also founded in the 19th Century and claimed that the world would come to an end in 1914. The fact that it obviously didn't has done nothing to stop missionaries world wide from knocking on people's doors and trying to recruit new members for their religion. I have to admire people who brave the potential hostility of strangers when they go door-to-door wanting to share their faith. I have had both Mormons and Jehovah's Witnesses come to my house. I usually ask them, "Is there any way I can prove to you that your religion is wrong?" They always stand firm and declare their religion to be the only true one. Then I say, "Then we have nothing to talk about."

As a college teacher, I had an experience with a student who said to me (referring to the popularity of teachers on campus), "I'm sick and tired of hearing students refer to you and Vic Burton as God." So help me, I resisted this retort as long as I could; but as she was finally getting up to leave, I said, "Peggy, Vic Burton is not God." She stopped breathing, narrowed her eyes, then gave me a "You've really gone too far this time" look.

If there is indeed a personal God who sees everything, I'm sure He was laughing his ass off.

Chapter Fourteen

Realization Number Eight

Doubting Religion or that God Exists is a Sign that You are Making Spiritual Progress

You are not "falling away" or wrapped in the devil's clutches whether your doubt is small or big. Jehovah might have had you stoned to death or threatened you with hell, but the point is Jehovah was not God. And if you doubt that, I suggest you read my book *Rico's Irreverent Bible Studies.* I wrote the book under the name Rico T. Scimassas because these Bible studies go after Jehovah with no holds barred and expose him for the psycho that he was.

Anyone who reads the *Old Testament* without a religious bias will have no problem with what I said in the last sentence.

The True God gave you a mind, and with that mind you are free to be open to the leanings of your soul. If you are part of an organized religion, that religion is more into telling you what to think rather than allowing you to think for yourself. At some time in your life – or perhaps even now – you experienced a discomfort about what you were told to believe, and perhaps – just perhaps – you felt a little bit guilty about it. You may have prayed that you be led back to the true path and given the strength to do it. The thing is that you just might be divinely nudged to the true path.

You are a unique individual; you have a unique personality, and you are being led toward what the Swiss psychiatrist Carl Gustav Jung referred to as self-fulfillment. There are very few churches that concern themselves with self-fulfillment or what psychiatrist Abraham Maslow referred to as "self-realization" (his original term, also commonly used, was "self-actualization.") In fact, if you use these terms around true believers, they will come up with some terms of their own: humanism, new age thought, etc. Either way, they are suggesting that you are walking away from the fold and need to be straightened out as much as possible. People will pray that you come away from your "temptations" and get back into the fold.

Your doubt just might be the voice for God or the Holy Spirit. For those who can't deal with terminology like this, there may be something higher within you urging you on to another path. Your doubt is real – don't stifle it or pray that it be removed from you. This is probably the best thing that could be happening to you, and I urge you to welcome it, because it is a sign that you are ready for something new and better. You are not under the wings of Lucifer. Satan doesn't have his hands around your throat. The devil is not victorious. In fact, if there is indeed a devil, his greatest victory on planet earth just might be organized religion.

"But I had such great comfort in my religion just a few years ago," you say. First of all, let me state that most people misunderstand the true meaning of comfort. Comfort comes from two Latin words: *cum* and *forte*. Even without a knowledge of Latin, you know words like "fortify" and "fortitude." These words suggest power, and that is what "cum forte" means: to be with power. So the doubt you are experiencing could actually be a gift, a sign that you are ready to move to something much higher. The fact that this never happened with your parents and grandparents is no reason for you to feel spiritually superior. They may have had their own doubts and gotten over them. In fact, this could easily happen to you if your need for acceptance by others outweighs the leanings of your own soul.

I began having those doubts when I was in seminary. Imagine my anguish when I said to my wife, "I don't know if I believe this stuff anymore. I can't go up to the pulpit and say Jesus will save you from sin and hell when I'm not even sure that Jesus was the son of God and whether hell exists." I was in hell while in seminary, and people avoided me. I understood the truism "the best place to lose your faith is in a seminary." So many times I wanted to scream out, "This is bullshit! I can't take it anymore!" In class, I was told by the professor, "Mr. Barranger, you are quickly walking away from the footsteps of Jesus."

The year was 1969, so the drug movement was in full gear. My advisor was one of the finest people I knew, so I approached him about doing an individual project on the theological implications of drugs. I mentioned that I would go down to the Boston common and back to the high school where I taught the previous year and write a paper on my conclusions. The fact is that this was one of the main experiences that would change my life. I had a former student claim that he came to believe in Jesus as the result of an LSD trip, but he was the rarity. Many told me that they felt the presence of God when they did mescaline, LSD, or mushrooms. Many offered to give me the material and guide me through the experience. However, I refused because I still believed that it was wrong and that I would have a bad experience. (Many years later, I eventually did hashish and mushrooms and found the experiences unique, yet still inferior to the Zen meditation that I was doing regularly.) I wrote my paper on the experiences I had and drew some conclusions from the experience. It became a rather lengthy paper on my research and I turned it in to my professor. After a month, I still did not have a grade for the project. I eventually called him and asked if there was a problem. He said, "I've been agonizing over this paper for a month. You certainly have done your research thoroughly, but I am thinking of two grades and only two grades... A or F." He eventually decided to give me an A, but not without a lot of doubt and anguish. It was years later that I realized that he had a strong evangelical paradigm and I was experiencing a paradigm shift.

Maybe this is what is happening to you. We are living in times of change and a paradigm shift is more easily seen now than it was in 1969.

Thus, if you are experiencing doubt, don't be hard on yourself. It just might be a cause for celebration.

Chapter Fifteen

Realization Number Nine

Heresy is not a Bad Word

He who believes in a system wears a blindfold.
—Robert Anton Wilson

Most people are prisoners of their own brains.
—Richard Bandler

Throughout history, the words "heretic" and "heresy" have received very bad press. In some circles, these two words are used respectively with "evil one" and "evil." The words "heretic" and "heresy" can make such an emotional impact that some people will alter their very beliefs in order to avoid this label. Being called a heretic is something to be avoided. To engage in heresy is too often interpreted as meaning that one has "fallen away" or "departed from the true path."

This highly limited perception of heresy and heretics persists despite the fact that Jesus, Mohammed, Gautama Buddha, and virtually all "founders" of the world's religions were considered heretics in their own time. Buddha departed from the confining strains of his Hindu faith by claiming that our thoughts determined our reality. Jesus upset the Pharisees by daring to suggest that some of the Pharisees' laws were more limiting than spiritual. He also promoted unpopular ideas like loving your enemies and pursuing a lifestyle other than what your parents had determined for you.

Sadly, people use labels like heretic and heresy to manipulate others in the name of Jesus, Mohammed, and Buddha (as well as the core people of other world religions). This sets up a most interesting paradox: one is labeled a heretic when one appears to be departing from the statutes of his or her religion. However, careful scrutiny reveals that one is probably being called a heretic because he or she is blazing trails into an even deeper spiritual experience. Most are caught up in the chains of a religion that was inspired by and founded upon the work of an original heretic.

For those who are confused by the last statement, let's provide an example. John Hus was one of the first church leaders to suggest that people should be able to read the Bible in their own language (Czechoslovakian). However, the Church fathers were very threatened by this. They wanted to be guardians of the "Holy Word" and did not want the common people to be able to read the Bible for themselves. Therefore, they branded John Hus a heretic.

During long sessions at the Council of Constance (1416-1418), Hus gave more than thirty references from the scriptures themselves, which suggested that what was considered the word of God should be read by the people. The leaders of the Council of Constance all agreed with the scriptural validity of the references made by Hus. Despite this, John Hus was burned at the stake.

Why? Because the leaders determined that he was a heretic.

What Exactly is a Heretic?

The stifling of the individual may well be the stifling of the God in man.
                                        —Sri Aurobindo

We fear our highest possibilities. We are generally afraid to become that which we can glimpse in our most perfect moments, under condi-tions of great courage. We enjoy and even thrill to the godlike possi-bilities we see in ourselves and in such peak moments. And yet we simultaneously shiver with weakness, awe, and fear before those very same possibilities.   —Abraham Maslow

The word "heretic" comes from the Greek and simply means "one who chooses." A heretic is one who chooses what he will believe – and eventually moves to a level of mental freedom where he no longer needs beliefs to dominate his spiritual experience. In no way is a person a heretic (the old negative form) if she chooses to believe something other than what she has been taught by her culture, society, or church. However, a person is a heretic (the good form) if she chooses beliefs other than what she has been taught. In essence, she is saying, "I am choosing a new level of experience because my old experience is neither satisfying or meaningful."

In this context, the person is not a heretic because he believes something different from what is considered "the truth" or "the only way." Instead, a person becomes a heretic when he begins making choices for himself based on his experience and spiritual exploration. This means that not only is heresy a good idea, it also means that heresy is essential in the spiritual quest of each individual human being.

If a heretic is one who chooses, then heresy is the act of choice. Heresy is not evil. Nor is it something that is a part of falling away from the truth. Actually, heresy is an essential part of marching toward the truth. Heresy is an indication that a person is ready to begin giving up his conditioned beliefs and is ready to choose new ways of perception based on his experiences and his exploration.

A Call for Heresy

We are not trapped in some kind of original sin; only original stupidity. Any stupidity can be overcome by a determined effort of intelligence.   —Ron Smothermon

The lover is a psycho-spiritual outlaw, free of all cultural taboos, yet profoundly responsible.
            —Robert A. Masters from *The Way of the Lover*

The world does not need people who are faithful to the doctrines of the faith that they are expected to maintain and nurture.

Instead, the world needs people who will move from their very safe comfort zones and actively pursue heresy. Despite all the noises made about how great the religious experience is, it actually remains a force for the conditioning of the mind rather than the release of the mind. Thus, spiritual growth and mental development require that a person move from conditioned beliefs and attitudes and begin the process of making saner choices.

Thus, this is a call for heresy. It is a plea for people to break free from the chains of their religious conditioning and seek a path based on experience rather than dogma or replayed archetypes. (Jung claimed that archetypes are mental sets deep within us that make a powerful impact upon our lives. These are very old and have been influencing us for thousands of years.)

If Buddha could see the ritualistic and mental demands placed on people in the Buddhist faith today, he would probably weep. Here is a religious leader who made a point of stilling and emptying his mind. Yet, if he were here today, he would find the monks of his faith engaging in raping minds with the expectation of Herculean feats of memory and rigid ritual. (I am aware that much of this ritual has the intention of emptying, stilling, or liberating the mind; however, much of the original purpose has been lost in the development of dogma and religion.)

If Jesus Christ could see the religious "litigation" that has blossomed in his name, he might be tempted to step forward and say, "I don't remember saying that dancing was sinful." He also might say, "In addition to urging that an adulteress sin no more, I also did not judge her. I suggest that you do the same." To people who limit themselves and somehow convince themselves that this highly limited life is spiritual, Jesus said, "I have come that you might have life and have it more abundantly." (John 10:10)

Jesus was not only a heretic, he also called people to choose a better way (in other words, "to be a heretic"). The call for heresy is not something instituted by this writer as much as it has been by the spiritual trail-blazers of the past. They were "divine ass-kickers" who wanted people to move from their sleep to a new level of waking – moving up to better and more effective choices. The call for heresy is not something new; it is something that has been forgotten by people who have become so comfortable with their religious indoctrination that they fail to realize that their religion is supposed to "shake things up" and move them to even better choices.

Consider Being a Divine Heretic

Those who are asleep to their true nature cannot be trusted, for they are strangers to their integrity.   —Robert A. Masters

The tragedy with most religious doctrines is that they focus more on dogma than spiritual experience. In one of those most ironic of intentions, the pursuit of the "right doctrine" actually prevents spiritual experience. The obsession for the "right beliefs" is an insurance policy against experiencing God. By limiting one's religious experience to one hour a week on a pre-established day, the poor Holy Spirit (or High Self) is strangled in what it can do.

The heretic is not limited to a pre-digested belief system. He also is not limited to a certain way of experiencing God. Nor is he stuck in the extremely naive idea that all spiritual experiences have to feel good or happen within his limited paradigm. Like the spiritual leader and writer Joel Goldsmith, the heretic says, "Let me experience the breadth of the spiritual experience and then make choices based on those experiences." The heretic does not choose in advance a pre-digested group of beliefs and then "demand" that his future experiences fall within those beliefs. Instead, he remains open to choose what he thinks might be the truth based on his own experiences with God, his Higher Self, the Holy Spirit, the Dynamic Ground, the Force, the God beyond God, Brahman, or any other spiritual force capable of leading one from sleep into a state of becoming awake.

Those Who are Terrified of Heretics

Powerful churches, political parties, and vested financial interests have a strong desire to program the rest of us into the particular "Real" universes that they find profitable, and to keep us from becom - ing self-programmers. They want to "take responsibility" for us, and they do not want us to "take responsibility" for ourselves.
        —Robert Anton Wilson

Since the birth of religion, we have always had a "ruling priest class" that has stood ready to tell us what the true faith is and which beliefs are deemed acceptable. What has kept this ruling priest class alive are the millions of people who want to be told what the true way is and what to believe. They want their religion or faith to be like a TV dinner that simply needs to be slipped into the oven – with little thought or preparation necessary. Like the TV dinner, these religions or faiths are highly processed and almost totally lacking in any nourishment. They merely pander to the comfort of those who are terrified to choose. In other words, those who are too frightened to be true heretics have chosen for themselves a falsely comfortable way of learning about and relating to God.

There's just one problem with all of this: God often has a hard time getting through the barriers of these processed religions. Because people demand that their religious experience happen within their limited paradigms, they set up very narrow ways of experiencing God, the Holy Spirit, and divine guidance that can come from within. (Jesus did say that the Kingdom of God was within us.)

Yet, people who break free from their cultural and religious conditioning are threatening to people who have chosen the conditioned religious approach. In fact, the closer the heretic moves toward experiencing God, the more the majority of people feel that this person is actually falling away from God. In a pompously paradoxical perversion, they pray that this heretical person will quickly return to the fold. Ironically, it is actually "the fold" that has prevented the emerging heretic from experiencing a closer relationship with God.

Many a well-meaning person will sit down with a someone and – with the sincerest of intentions – urge that someone to return to the old conditioned way of approaching God. The one urging the return assures the emerging heretic that the old way is best – even though that way no longer works (nor will it ever again work) for the emerging heretic.

That's why this "emerging" person must become a heretic: his past ways and conditioned responses no longer work. He needs to strike out and choose a better way. Despite the fact that he is upsetting parents, family members, and friends, he must leap into a space where he is free to make choices. If he does not have the freedom to make choices, his spiritual growth will be stunted, and he will only have "more of the same" for spiritual nourishment. In other words, his "return to the fold" practically insures that he will have little or no spiritual nourishment.

What he will get is merely the "satisfaction" of "knowing" that he is no longer a threat to the people in his fold. This is almost always a devastating price to pay on the spiritual quest.

Why the Heretical Path is Essential

When the walls are down, the world can expand. And that is the difference between a world that could be a heaven and one that becomes a hell.   —Deepak Chopra

The heretical path is essential because it is the only path with genuine choice. Other paths have pre-digested dogma and pre-selected beliefs as expectations. A person could have a genuine spiritual experience at a Billy Graham rally. However, instead of leaving the person's spiritual growth to the Holy Spirit, well-meaning people guide this "new convert" into an extremely narrow range of things to do that center more on dogma than experience.

The "new convert" will be told that only her freshly discovered path leads to eternal life. She will be told that she must study only the scriptures of this new found faith, that other scriptures are not true...

and are, perhaps, even evil. She will be told that she must read those scriptures faithfully – thus brainwashing herself to accept the dogmas of this "new religion." If she encounters something in the Bible that suggests reincarnation, she will be told that entertaining such a notion is not spiritually correct. She will be shown "the way," and God help her if the Holy Spirit leads her in another direction.

The heretical path is essential because it keeps the human soul open for choices – choices that are more aligned with holiness and divinity than religion or doctrine. The heretical path keeps a person's options open so that divine guidance can flourish instead of being stifled "in the name of the Lord." It allows people to tap into and nurture the divine spark within instead of looking to a pre-established set of concepts that may have little to do with God or anything Godly. The heretical path allows humans to look within for God rather than depending on ancient or rigid rituals that have become overrated with the passing of time.

The heretical path allows a person to question beliefs that were instilled when a person was too young to question them. The idea of dying for one's faith can become so induced into a child's religious upbringing that the heretical idea of living one's life abundantly may actually take a back seat to a "dying for the Lord" mentality. A child may become so ingrained with the idea that God frowns on sex that she may not be able to enjoy sex once she is married. A teenager may be so obsessed with wanting to please the god of his conditioning that he may never explore better ways to experience the True God. A person who sincerely and truly wants to serve God may think the only effective ways to do this would be to become an orthodox minister or a missionary. The heretical path helps people get beyond these stultifying limitations and opens the door for a much more fulfilling and spiritual way of living.

Heresy is not something evil blocking the human experience. It is actually an essential part of the human experience.

Chapter Sixteen
Realization Number Ten

When You Become a Heretic, You Move from Spiritual Slavery to Spiritual Liberation

I always thought that if something isn't working, that it might be an indication that it was time to do something else. If you know that some - thing doesn't work, then anything else has a chance of working than more of the same thing. —Richard Bandler

What Exactly is Spiritual Slavery?

One is in a state of spiritual slavery when he or she feels that beliefs about the divine are more important than experiencing the divine. Most organized religions make the claim that a person must pursue certain spiritually correct beliefs. Many organized religions claim that a failure to possess the right beliefs will lead to eternal damnation or a separation from God. Ironically, it is the possession of beliefs that contributes to a separation from God. Beliefs are baggage that prevent genuine efforts to develop a relationship with the true God.

One is in a state of spiritual slavery when she feels that being right is more important than realizing truth. Most organized religions are much more concerned with telling someone what they consider to be the truth. They have it pre-digested so that exploration is "no longer necessary." Thus, instead of a soul-wrenching search for the truth, the Twenty-first Century human merely needs to "find the correct TV dinner, plop it into the oven, and wait thirty minutes."

Being well conditioned and thoroughly brainwashed becomes much more important than becoming aware or becoming awake. In fact, most organized religions rarely provide experiences that increase awareness or move a person out of a state of being asleep. While most religion is well intended, it still is basically aligned with brainwashing and indoctrination. Because of this highly conditioned state of mind, heresy eventually becomes an essential part of spiritual liberation.

Heresy restores choice to the human experience. It says, "No matter what you have learned, you must allow your mind and your own personal experience to determine what works best for you."

The heretic realizes that God created each person as a unique human being and does not need his creations to fit into a cookie-cutter type of religion. Each human is supplied with a mind capable of grasping the distinction between what works in his spiritual experience and what is merely acceptable. Because humans are such "belonging-oriented" creatures, too many would rather "belong to the 'right' religion" than determine for themselves what spiritual experiences work best in their lives. The idea that such a thing as a right religion exists represents a part of conditioning established more than 4,000 years ago. That idea was part of a conditioning process that was meant to manipulate humanity into a state of spiritual slavery. (This idea is discussed in much greater depth in *Past Shock: The Origin of Religion and Its Devastating Impact on the Human Soul,* which can be ordered from The Book Tree, whose 800 number is on the back cover of this book).

That conditioning process continues today in the form of organized religion, the concept that there could be only one right religion, and the counterproductive idea that one must pursue religious beliefs rather than spiritual experiences. This conditioning process has created a highly refined form of spiritual slavery. Many people in this mind-set turn the spiritual quest into a deepening of spiritual slavery. They remain spiritual slaves because they have been effectively conditioned to feel good about their brainwashing and other experiences that only deepen that brainwashing. By continuing to insist that a right religion must exist, they continue to condition themselves to embrace the lies that they were told more than 4,000 years ago by forces that used organized religion as a means of exploiting newly created humans rather than liberating them.

Therefore, this call for heresy is not a plea. It is a clarion call to wake up from the sleep-induced conditioning of the past. While that conditioning was very powerful, it is permanent only if it is constantly reinforced. While constant reinforcement is the choice of the majority of humans, it does not have to be your choice. Heresy allows you to stand outside of your conditioning and allow your own experiences to determine what works and what doesn't. (Interestingly enough, the word "ecstasy" originally meant "to stand outside of.") Heresy also allows you to bring choice back into your experiences as a personal factor in creating your own spiritual liberation.

One begins the process of spiritual liberation by making the choice to pursue matters of genuine spiritual exploration instead of using personal energy to deepen the process of religious conditioning and brainwashing. This spiritual freedom comes from making choices based on personal revelation instead of acquired beliefs. Spiritual liberation will not happen until a person is free to make a choice. Sadly, few people are free to make choices until they are able to stand apart from the conditioning they had as a child.

While genuine spiritual experience is always liberating, it isn't always initially edifying. We are very well-conditioned creatures who desperately "need to believe." Thus, we will think that spiritual exploration and spiritual freedom lie in moving from one set of beliefs to yet another set of beliefs. This rarely works because it is more like changing the label on an empty bottle. Taking this analogy one step further, moving from one set of beliefs to yet another set of beliefs is like pouring new wine into old wineskins.

Heresy and the Dark Night of the Soul
The Dark Night as a Sign of Coming Spiritual Liberation

I have no intention of giving sanction to a new edition of the old fiasco.   —Satprem

*Whenever you get confused, you can get excited about the new under -
standing that awaits you.* —Sri Aurobindo

Too often, people during the process of shifting from a belief-
dominant paradigm to an experience-based paradigm encounter what
the Hindu's refer to as a "dark night of the soul." During this "dark
night of the soul," one feels a sense of emptiness. Nothing seems to
work anymore. While this "dark night of the soul" may not feel good,
it is almost always an indication that something good is happening.
Instead of something appearing not to work, what happens is that the
spiritual seeker wakes up to the fact that very little in his religious
experience has *ever* worked.

Most people want to avoid this form of spiritual cleansing
because it doesn't feel good. Yet something deep within us is saying,
"Your old way isn't working anymore." This force within us is much
closer to God, the Holy Spirit, and our true selves. This force within us
wants to work for us. However, the majority of us would rather have
comfort and certainty. Spiritual awareness and truth are rare goals in
the ranks of the believers.

Yet, deep within us something wants to blot out the false light
and move us closer to the light of truth. For most people, this appears
to be darkness – perhaps even evil. It isn't. Instead, something deep
within us wants to burn away the spiritual dross. Moreover, with such
an essential cleansing, the eyes of the soul are cleared to pursue greater
truths. In many of the far Eastern cultures, the "dark night of the soul"
is a badge of honor – an indication that this person is ready to move to
a higher level.

However, in America, the "dark night of the soul" is too often
not seen as a badge of honor. The majority of Americans see the "dark
night of the soul" as something to be numbed, overcome, or "cured."
At the point in which God is saying, "I want to move you forward,"
the religiously devout are praying that this liberation be exorcised.
Valium, that little blue or yellow pill, is used to numb this essential

heretical crisis. Therapists are sought to free them from the healing impulse that is welling up inside of them like a volcano. With the "dark night of the soul," God is stirring things up so that spiritual advancement becomes a priority.

A Call for an Escape from Beliefs

We are not trapped in some kind of original sin; only original stupidity. And stupidity can be overcome by a determined effort of intelligence. —Colin Wilson

Beliefs will not liberate us. They simply don't have the power to do that. All beliefs can do is weigh people down and make the spiritual quest more of a struggle than the dance that it was intended to be. Beliefs have no intrinsic way of leading people to the truth. Only personal experience can do that. Buddha did not tell his followers to believe in him. He urged people to work out their own salvation.

In Christianity, the issue is a little more sticky. Salvation appears to be wedged deeply into the idea that one must believe in Jesus Christ in order to be saved. In addition, we have the apostle Paul claiming that belief in Jesus was essential for salvation. Having these ideas burned into our minds at a very young age can be quite powerful. I even heard on a radio talk show that UFO's are here because this is the only planet where the aliens can attain salvation. No one wants to burn in hell. Therefore, the pursuit of belief becomes more like a form of insurance than of a genuine spiritual experience.

The problem with such dogma is that it comes from "gospels" that were written at least a hundred years after the death of Jesus. They were highly edited to insure that they would fit into an already structured belief system. This belief system was also highly influenced by the Jewish belief system of which Jesus was a part. Rather than create spiritual liberation, these belief systems have contributed to a spiritual slavery. These rigid belief systems have created spiritual anguish for many and spiritual certainty for those who want a pre-digested belief system. The end result is spiritual harm and a propensity to have spiritual experience blocked rather than nurtured.

Heresy helps people get free from stultifying beliefs. It allows people to use their God-given freedom to search for a greater truth. It frees people from the idea that there must be one true religion and one spiritually correct set of beliefs. Heresy allows us to keep the power of choice alive. It helps us get beyond an ancient programming that was manipulative and inducing of slavery. In one of the greatest ironies, heresy allows us to break free of the conditioning of a false god and be free to search for and experience the God beyond this false god. To search for the true God, one rapidly comes to the conclusion that he must become a heretic.

Sadly, the majority of humans are stuck in their slave conditioning. They would rather be "certain" than free. The quest for certainty stifles the human spirit and chokes the human soul. Certainty and "being right" may feel good, but it rarely does any good. Certainty brings the spiritual quest to a dead stop and causes the mind to rest in sleep-driven comfort rather than pursuing a path more aligned with nurturing the soul. The best antidote for all of this is an infusion of heresy.

Heresy: The Way to Personal and Spiritual Liberation

The seeker will discriminate between those things that tend to blur his vision and those which clarify it; such essentially will be his "morali - ty." —Sri Aurobindo

Spiritual liberation is the goal of any human wanting to experience God. However, this spiritual liberation demands that the seeker move apart from "safe" and "certain" beliefs that have been weighing him down. The move beyond this stultifying, belief-dominated certainty is a move toward heresy. Heresy is not meant to destroy religion as much as it is meant to nudge the human soul toward experiencing God in a more meaningful way.

Ironically, it is the Holy Spirit that leads one from paths that are blocking the experience of God. The Holy Spirit is not a destroyer, because that is not its nature. Instead, it nudges us deep at the soul level and urges us to gently put aside all of the false comfort of the past. This way, one can pursue a path with greater heart and greater possibilities of awakening.

Thus, this call for heresy is not about destruction or ridicule of what is past. Usually, the self-induced slavery of the past inspires a greater desire for genuine spiritual liberation. The heretic is not one who shouts in the streets. The heretic is instead a catalyst for spiritual growth. As he or she becomes more free, so are others able to move closer to spiritual liberation.

Chapter Seventeen

Walking the Path of Religious Freedom:

Pointers for a Successful Journey

I assume that you have read all the realizations and some of you might be asking yourself, "How come I don't feel more free? I read the realizations." Actually, you have begun a process which will free you from religion and put you on the path where you can make more choices (and thus become a divine heretic). I include this final chapter to give you some pointers on how your journey can be more successful. Rarely does a person finish a book like this and want to go out into the streets screaming, "I'm free!"

However reading the book did plant some powerful seeds – seeds which will grow into religious freedom.

There are four levels which you could possibly experience on your journey, and being aware of them could move you along.

The lowest of the levels is LEVEL ONE. That is the level of the religious fanatic. A LEVEL ONE person is so locked into his or her religion that getting free of it is highly improbable.

The LEVEL TWO person is dedicated to his or her religion, but he or she feels a "gnawing" deep from within that there is some-thing higher.

The LEVEL THREE person knows that he is not standing on solid ground when it comes to his religion. He knows that something is wrong and he can't shake that feeling. Although, it is not a good feeling, it is a great step forward in making spiritual practice. The illusions are beginning to fall away, and that explains why you feel disillusioned.

The LEVEL FOUR person is most of the time at peace with his or her newly chosen path, despite any pressure from friends, family, etc. He is no longer looking for the true religion or a new belief system. The choices made almost always lead to a higher level of being.

In ancient China a story is told of a boy of sixteen who ran to his father in tears because his horse had run away. His father, a very wise man, said, "Son, don't judge." The next day the horse came back with three new horses. The boy ran to his father and said, "This is wonderful, I now have three more horses!" Still the father said, "Son, don't judge." The next day the boy was breaking in one of the new horses. He fell off and broke his leg. While lying in bed with great pain, he said, "Father, this is awful, this is the worst thing that has ever happened to me! "The father once again said, "Son, don't judge." The following day a group of war lords came through the village taking with them every able-bodied young man. They looked at the boy and decided that he couldn't help them. "Father this is wonderful," the boy exclaimed. "Breaking my leg was the best thing that could have ever happened to me." Once again the father said, "Son, don't judge." Then he added: "None of us yet knows enough to be able to make judgment on any person or any event. If we don't have all the facts, we waste our energy making judgments."

Transformation

The key to freeing your soul is the courage and wisdom to allow a natural and transformational experience to happen. The problem is that you might have lost touch with what is best for you.

When your horse is dead, get off it.   —Native American proverb

You might have become comfortable with ideas and habits which block your personal transformation. Too often, what is meaningful and natural to the human experience is seen as frightening. Yet this experience can be your greatest ally.

This higher level of experience is meant to break you free from conditioning and habits that no longer serve you. This experience is meant to lead you from what is both comfortable and stultifying and guide you toward your soul's purpose: a personal function where you will effortlessly experience greater spiritual awareness – not dreams that come from your society and its conditioning.

Most people are willing – and even expect – to struggle for spiritual progress because they cannot tell the difference between real dreams and conditioned dreams. There's a very simple test to tell which is which. Your conditioned dreams require great amounts of effort and struggle – *your real dreams don't.*

You don't have to work that hard to figure it out. Your freed soul will take you into the higher experience when you're ready for it. If you are reading this book, you are most likely ready. This is one of the most beautiful things about these higher experiences. Your soul is guiding this experience. It knows the time and place for moving you to the next and more fulfilling level of your life.

You may have become disillusioned with what you have been doing in your life. Your job no longer provides the same satisfaction. Increasingly, you look forward to the weekends. Your weekend worship doesn't give you the same edification. In fact, you might find that you are even more discontented. You have been saying, "There's got to be a better way," and you are saying it more often.

What had given you meaning and pleasure before now appears to be empty. The sports you enjoyed, the parties that once stimulated you, and the hobbies which provided a sense of fulfillment are now banal and fail to give you pleasure.

Many of your friends no longer strike you as being as interesting or nurturing. People you looked forward to getting together with for the weekend now provide lower levels of interest and stimulation.

You might even be to the point where you still get together with these people, but when you are with them, you wish you were someplace else.

You are experiencing a wonderful purification. On the physical level, you've experienced purifications before. The problem is that you might have called these purifications "sickness." When your body purges itself of toxins, you rarely feel good. However, you eventually feel better – and actually get better – once the toxins are gone.

In this experience, you come to realize that you have mental toxins also. The problem is, these are much more "accepted" and tolerated than the physical toxins. Sadly, many of us might actually be conditioned to believe that these mental toxins are a natural part of life. While they might be typical, they are not natural. Yet, for some, getting rid of them might cause some discomfort. In one of the greatest ironies of the human experience, our physical body does much better than our mind in getting rid of physical toxins.

Even though our soul is driving us to move to something better, we too often surrender to those mental toxins – even when they attempt to convince us that we are not worthy of a more fulfilling life. These toxic mental scripts that often appear and block our spiritual progress include:

I could never do that.

I might have been able to do that when I was younger, but I'm too old now.

How would I look if I did that?

It would be irresponsible for me to do that.

There I go, being silly thinking about that.

Whatever "that" is doesn't matter. It could be moving to a more meaningful job, moving to a better place to live, or looking at your life from a totally different perspective. Level Three is a wake up call from your soul. It is not conditioned by society, school, or family values. Your soul knows what will give you the most fulfillment, success, and prosperity, and – if you will listen and follow its leadings – will move you to this new level quickly and effectively.

Trust this **higher** level of experience. Despite what the mental toxins might suggest, there is nothing crazy about it. This new level has a number of very sane rules. One of them is:

What isn't working for you anymore we are going to remove.

If you allow it, your soul will gently and effectively take you to a better way of living that will provide higher levels of life experience.

While the inner you, your soul, has great wisdom in what to eliminate, our conditioned minds almost always put up a fight. Old ideas die hard, and they do begin to die during entry at Level Three.

LET THEM DIE.

They will no longer serve you. In fact they will block your becoming who you uniquely are. Holding on to these ancient and devastating ideas will insure that you will have to continue struggling for diminishing levels of success.

There are seven basic rules for getting the most benefit from the freedom experience. Each will help you move thorough it quickly. Even better, utilizing these guidelines will help you enjoy one of the most exciting moments of your life – freeing of your soul.

RULE NUMBER ONE

Accept That Any Discomfort You Have Might Be Working for You

First, you had better understand the word "comfort." It comes from two Latin words: "cum forte." Literally, this means "with power." Once again, it is one of the great ironies of the human experience: a word that once meant empowerment now means something closer to relaxation, security, or being sedentary.

If you just let your experience happen, it will empower you.

Consider that your comfort might lie with something that is blocking you. *That is the only way that you could be experiencing dis - comfort with something that is liberating you.*

RULE NUMBER TWO

Accept That You Are Moving to Something Better

While this might appear to be like the first rule, it has a different thrust. You may not feel as coordinated, as lucid, as together as you did before. In many ways you might feel disillusioned.

Disillusionment is exactly what is happening to you. All of the illusions in your life that were centered around heavily conditioned lies are being dissolved. With disillusionment eventually comes a lifestyle without the ego's illusions.

However, with most people disillusionment simply doesn't feel that way. It rarely feels good. Most in the human race have become very comfortable with illusions – even those that hinder the human experience. Thus, when these illusions finally begin to dissolve, your initial response may be more fear than joy. Most people at Level Three first feel like they want their illusions back.

Some quickly decide to return to Level Two, and this is sometimes a good idea and will be discussed later in this chapter.

RULE NUMBER THREE

Accept That You've Been Badly Conditioned About Crisis

You will deal with your crisis better if you know that it is actually working for you. Realize how many people "get through" their crises by taking Valium, overeating, seeking more sensual pleasures, or finding more exciting diversions. If you are really fortunate, none of these things will work for you. That is one way to know that you are in the freedom experience: what diversions, therapies, and other areas that had worked for you before will be less effective.

Realize that you most likely don't need therapy. You are experiencing therapy – and it's free.

You are not pressured to follow some therapist's latest discovery or be a subject for his next article for a journal. This soul level therapy is tailor-made for you and done for you at the deepest level of your soul. It will always work in your best interests.

RULE NUMBER FOUR

Accept That a Personal Re-alignment Is Taking Place

If you drove a car in which the front wheels were dreadfully out of line, you would experience quite a shift when you finally had the wheels aligned. With the car, the shift is very pleasant.

Not so with the human mind.

Thanks to cultural conditioning, you have been forced out of alignment with your soul's purpose. You have been listening to voices outside of you instead of your soul's voice. When the alignment is complete, your system of intuition will work much more effectively. You will hear those gentle intuitive whisperings which will guide you to much higher levels of fulfillment, success, and abundance. These gut feelings lead to opportunity and require much less effort.

The price you have to pay for this is very small.

RULE NUMBER FIVE

Remember That You Are Burning Off the Dross

It is more than just a re-alignment that you are experiencing. You are actually experiencing a purification. If you allow yourself to ride out this experience, you will function with far greater efficiency.

What is this dross? It is the ideas and personally conditioned life patterns which stand in the way of your personal fulfillment.

What you previously thought would work for you is now falling away. You might feel a sense of loss. But you will gain in losing it.

If you have a lot of dross to burn, don't beat yourself up. It's not your fault. Nor is it the fault of those who conditioned you. They too had their conditioning. Forgive them and move on.

RULE NUMBER SIX

Accept That Going Back to Level Two Is Not Necessarily Going Backwards

If you return to a lower freedom level – as some do – you are not a failure. What's back there might feel good... for a while. However, you're going back to a lower level so that you can effectively process what you have learned in your journey to spiritual freedom.

Going back to a lower level gives the ego what it needs – a sense of security. This sense of security, however, is false, but your ego doesn't know that. All it knows is that you are experiencing something threatening. This is where you might want to trust the time/space reality of the soul. It knows that your ego is frightened. It also knows that you have to get beyond the leanings of your ego.

The Universe doesn't punish us; It just says, "Let's play it again."
—Paul Brenner

Should you feel you need to go back, the above quote is highly relevant. Sometimes circumstances change, and we need to retreat. There is no harm in this as long as you realize what you are doing, and realize that you want to go into the Level Three experience again.

There are many reasons why this can only be temporary. Your body, mind, and soul were created to help you grow. However, the high-powered antics of Level Two or the security blanket of Level One no longer have any relevance for you. Your past goals are limitations to the possibility of what you can be.

RULE NUMBER SEVEN

Accept That The Level Three Experience Can be Fun and Positively Challenging – Even if That Isn't Your First Impression.

Level Three was never meant to be miserable. It is meant to get you beyond a stultifying comfort which keeps your soul from working for you.

When we ride a rollercoaster, we know that the ride is going to be safe. We accept that our body will experience stress. But it's fun – as long as the ride stops. Yet the roller coaster ride as a diversion has very little potential for spiritual transformation.

The Level Three experience is an all but guaranteed transformation. And it can be fun.

Some people fail to enjoy this level because they are resisting it rather than flowing with it. The resistance comes from the strange yet necessary shifts that are occurring. While they are strange, they don't have to be uncomfortable.

If a pilot has been flying a boring route on automatic pilot for the past 100 flights, he might experience anxiety if the automatic pilot kicks off. But he has the option of accepting the challenge of flying the plane himself. He has the opportunity to fly a more creative route. However, he's not going to have any fun if he constantly whines about the failed automatic pilot.

You have the same option in Level Three. Your very boring, very counterproductive auto-pilot is shut off. Where you had limited options before, you now have some very exciting options.

There is free will in the universe. You have every right to get upset and experience anxiety and despair to the fullest. Your lower level "teddy bear" has been taken away, but your higher level one is waiting in the wings. Keep reminding yourself that the higher level teddy bear is much more fun to play with.

Anxiety is the dizziness of freedom.   —Soren Kierkegaard

It would be ludicrous to claim that anxiety is fun. However, if you can accept that your anxiety is a herald to a transformed and liberated you, you can gain a whole new perspective on your anxiety.

If your anxiety comes from resisting your transformation, it will be an unpleasant sensation. However, if you accept that your anxiety is indeed the "dizziness of freedom," there is no reason why it need be unpleasant. In fact, it can be the harbinger of a soul breaking loose to freedom.

You would not be experiencing any of the unpleasant effects of Level Three if something deep inside of you didn't realize that you were strong enough to endure the rigors of you and your soul's liberation.

All your life you have had highly complicated systems to keep you locked in struggle. Now you can trust something deep within you to point to a much better way.

Accept that your soul will guide you with its best timing in your unique circumstances. Once you are following your soul's guidance, your soul's freedom is inevitable.

Appendix A

Personal Biography

Those of you who read the spiritual biography at the end of The Origin of Religion and its Impact on the Human Soul *need to know that this is NOT a repeat of that same spiritual biography. I wanted to write something that I experienced and you, perhaps, could identify with. Although I talk about my younger years, I focus mainly on my experi- ence in seminary. You might find yourself identifying with some of the experiences I had. Otherwise skip this part of the book: it is not meant to be a main part of it.*

I really didn't start thinking much about God until I was about eight years old. My mother would be with me as I said my prayers, and I didn't have the gall to say, "I don't feel like praying tonight." Nor was I intellectually advanced enough to say, "He already knows what I want, so why bother praying?" I went to Sunday School and was bored out of my mind. After that my parents dragged me off to church – a double whammy for God every Sunday.

By the time I turned twelve, I was really having problems with regular school. I actually failed seventh grade and had to go to summer school and get passing grades in order to be admitted into eighth grade. It was in eighth grade that I had my experience of accepting Jesus as my personal savior. This was a good example of the conversion arche- type. I worked harder, and I would say that I passed with flying colors, but mostly I had C's and D's. I hated school and found it a most bor- ing experience. The problem was that I complained to my family and they, therefore, enrolled me in a recreation program at the school. I found that just as boring as my subjects in school.

100

Being "saved," I carried my Bible to school with me and placed it on top of my books. That was something that all the new born-again Christians were doing, so we eventually singled ourselves out as the newly born-again Christians.

Ninth grade was a disaster with the exception of one thing. I felt like God was calling me to be a minister of the gospel. It was a very strong feeling. Otherwise, I spent more time reading the Bible instead of doing my homework. To make a long story short, I failed ninth grade. I failed English, History, Algebra, and Latin: enough to insure that I would have to repeat the grade.

My second year in ninth grade started off with a bang. I got A's in Latin because I had already been through it. History was as boring as ever and I only got C's there. I got B's in the rest of my courses.

Still I felt a strong calling from God to become a minister.

I'm not going to explain much about my college experience. Among other things I managed to flunk out. If I went to summer school and maintained a high enough average, I would be allowed to come back for my junior year. How did I make it through my freshman year? I was a chemistry major studying to be a geo-chemist and was really enjoying the material, but was doing poorly in my required courses.

However, one night in summer school I had the epiphany of my life. Shakespeare was one of the courses which I was taking, and, as usual, I expected to be bored out of my mind. One of the early assigments was *Hamlet.* I read it expecting it to be like *Macbeth,* which had bored me in my senior year of high school. However, when I finished *Hamlet,* I realized that it had really touched me. At one in the morning I began reading it again and got just as much out of it the second time. I had nothing higher than a C in all of my required English *courses.*

However, that night I realized that I wanted to become an English teacher. The following morning I found Professor Sloane, and the conversation went like this:

Professor Sloane, I want to be an English major.

Good God, Mr. Barranger, that is the last major you should be picking.

I want to work with high school kids and teach them English.

Good God, I can't believe what I'm hearing.

I read *Hamlet* last night and really loved it. I want to teach kids to love literature.

Are you aware that you have to have a B average to be accepted as an English major?

But you can override that and accept me.

Heavenly day, I am probably going to regret this and make myself the laughing stock of the school, but I'm going to accept you. You just might have the makings of a good teacher.

Summing up, I graduated from Dickinson College (Carlisle, PA) and went on to teach six years of high school English. These were some of the most meaningful years of my life. I loved kids and teaching them was fun and fulfilling.

During the seventh year of teaching high school, I began feeling the calling to be a minister. I wanted to slough it off, because I was enjoying high school teaching so much. I was even enjoying the PTA meetings. But I felt that if I could become a youth minister I could be help kids even more and serve God in the process. This seemed like a good idea.

During the eighth year of teaching at East Lansing high school in Michigan, the calling became more intense. The year was 1968 – a year that America was going through great turmoil. I discussed "my calling" with a few ministers. One of the ministers came up with a good idea: take a year off from teaching and enroll in a seminary and see how I feel about the whole thing. Thus, I told my principal that I would be leaving at the end of the year to go to seminary. The Principal, Gerald Kusler, did not fight me and tell me that I should remain in teaching. Instead, he supported my decision – despite the fact that he had picked me as a teacher a group of mothers could observe as an example of good teaching.

Thus in the fall of 1968 I began my first year of seminary. I was excited. I was going to spend three years in seminary learning how to preach the gospel. I was elected president of my class and everything seemed to be going beautifully.

Then it happened.

George Noory, who puts on a late-night radio program, tells of an incident while driving where – despite the fact that the light was green – he had this strong message to slow down and stop. At that moment a large truck ran the red light. If George had not stopped, he would have been killled or hurt very badly.

The same thing was happening with me. In many ways I had a messsage to "slow down and stop." Despite all the good friends I was making, despite the fact that I was at the top of my Greek class, and despite the excellent rapport I had with my professsors, I had this uncomfortable feeling in the pit of my stomach that was telling me that something was wrong. I couldn't put my finger on it nor could I understand it; however, it was a very uneasy feeling.

I tried talking about this to some of my close friends. However, they became uneasy with me and in some cases avoided me. Some thought that the Devil had a prime candidate and was pulling out all the stops. At the time, my wife Mary was putting me through school and our marrriage was doing fine. I drank wine to calm myself down, but it helped very little. In a way one might say that I was going through a "dark night of the soul."

I had one pathetic means to ease the pain. While lying in bed I would tell her the dirtiest jokes that I knew, and we would laugh together. This appeared to be a rebellion against what was making me feel so miserable. Other things followed.

I then began asking "embarrassing" questions in class. The following dialogue represents one of these. It begins with Professor Irving:

One thing you can count on: God never changes his mind.

Professor Irving, there was at least one time in the Old Testament that God changed his mind. God had mentioned that he was going to kill a certain man that night, and Isaiah convinved God that he should let him live longer. God came back to Isaiah and told Isaiah that He (God) would let the man live for another fifteen years. Now that sounds like God had actually changed His mind.

Mr. Barranger, God did not change his mind; he repented his decision.

Professor Irving, that is semantic crap.

Professor Irving never seemed to like me after that conversation. However, as I have mentioned before, some of the finest men I have met in my life were the professors in that seminary.

This did not stop me from asking pointed questions in class. With a visiting professor in Professor Irving's class, I asked another question, and Professor Irving apologized on my behalf immediately.

The visiting professor jumped on Irving right away.

> This is seminary. This is where those kind of questions should be asked. This is the place where things like this need to be worked out. What if he were to be asked a question like this in a Bible study?

> After class Professor Irving walked up to me and said the following:

> Mr. Barranger, you are walking further and further from the footsteps of Jesus.

When I returned thirteen years later for a visit to the seminary, Professor Irving was the only professor I saw. He said to me, " I just got back from San Diego where I attended the Bible inerrancy conference. I am convinced beyond any doubt that there are no errors in the Bible."

I had heard that there were at least 1,800 inconsistencies in the Bible, but I decided to say nothing.

I wrote a few notes to some of my favorite professors and then left the site.

Getting back to my time in seminary, I had one of the lowest days of my life. I was in the cafeteria getting my lunch and sat down with a group of people who were in my Greek class. One at the table stood up and said the following:

> Jack, will you please find another table to sit at? I just can't take you anymore.

> I ate alone...very depressed.

It was that weekend that I began crying uncontrollably. I was at the nadir of my seminary experience. I began to feel that if something looked good to me, I was under the influence of the devil.

And something was beginning to look good to me.

In my Church History class, we were not only given reading assignments but also asked to read a few hundred pages on our own. Since we were discussing the heresies of Christianity, I figured that I would read ideas that made no sense to Christianity. That's when *Gnosticism* slipped into my life. First of all, Gnosticim, in its general form, was in existence long before Christianity. It believed that God did not create the earth but that this was the work of the Demiurge, an imperfect creator. In fact, it states that the entire Universe was created by the Demiurge. Evidently, the Demiurge did not have all his marbles, and that is why some Gnostics refer to him as the Crazy Creator.

However, what impressed me most about Gnosticism was the fact that it was more important to know God than to believe in him. When I brought this up in class some would turn around and give me dirty stares. I even heard someone whisper,

Oh, Lord, it's Barranger again.

Each day I would wake up dreading going to school. I found in the *Gospel According to the Trailians* a reference stating that in the final days men would ingest substances that would change their consciousness. I brought this up in class and the professor decided to dismiss class ten minutes early, making fun of me in the process. A couple of days later I showed him the passage, and could see that he was impressed, but he never mentioned any of this to the class. Thus I was to continue as the class reprobate.

One day on the way to class, Howard Keely, one of my professors, stopped me on the way to Church History and said, "Come on up to my office. Let's talk."

I can't remember the exact date, but this was the day of my second epiphany. This was a good one, which took me higher than any drug that I could take or have taken. His words I remember almost word for word:

> Jack, don't go into the pastoral ministry. You're going to be miserable there. Why don't you return to teaching and make your students your congregation?

I protested at first, mentioning that I felt called by God to go into the ministry.

> Jack, your classses can be your ministry. I have a daughter who's in ninth grade, and I know that this teacher has done more for her than any minister. She raves about him. She talks about him all the time. She is a better person because of this teacher.

I began to feel a load dropping from my soul as we continued with the conversation. Dr. Keely was making the leap because he sensed that my going into the pastoral ministry would be a disaster.

The more that I argued for going into the youth ministry, the more he convinced me that I would be most effective with regular kids. The conversation lasted for over an hour, and when I walked out of his office I was a free man. My fellow students looked friendlier. My drive home was like riding a bus to freedom. I couldn't wait to talk about it with my wife.

She burst into tears, but these were tears of relief. The problem was that I had to finish the semester before I would be eligible for a Masters in Theology. This was sixteen semester hours before I could get the degree. I wanted to get the degree just in case I wanted to *real-ly* punish myself and get a Master of Divinity – requiring another year and a half of schooling.

That's when I had my third epihany. I woke up one morning with a brilliant idea: Why couldn't I work off those sixteeen hours by travelling and writing about those travels? I was able to do this. My main travel was spending five weeks in Israel and visiting the places where Jesus walked. Another four hours was conferred by interviewing Danish mininsters about Christ's resurrection and writing a paper synthesizing their ideas. I spoke and understood Danish, and got to meet a lot of interesting people; not to mention the delicious food we enjoyed when we were asked to stay for dinner. It is considered bad form in Denmark if you are invited to dinner and refuse. One other Danish tradition was that when several plates of pastry are placed in front of you, it is considered bad form if you don't eat at least one of each pastry. (My mouth waters as I write this: the Danes sure know how to make good pastry.)

The third way to work off four hours was to go to Switzerland and spend a month at the L'abri Fellowship. This was a place where Christians and non-Christians could come together and learn about religion. I would also write a paper about this experience.

The fourth way to make it to sixteen hours was a strange one: I read about 30 books that were written for young evangelical Christians and agreed to write a report on my findings. This, in many ways, was a minor epiphany. Not only were there a series of inconsistencies in the books, but much of the writing was horrible. One author thought that God was trying to tell a certain boy something when his foot got caught in a fender, and was dragged on his back for nearly a mile. The author simply assumed that God was telling this young boy that he was "backsliding."

What all of this did for me was uplifting. No more dirty looks came when I wanted to ask a question because I wasn't there, cooped up in a classroom. And when finished with these journeys I still had decided to take Dr. Keely's advice and return to teaching. It just seemed like a good idea. In Israel, my wife and I got to walk in the same places where Christ walked. The discussion with Danish ministers was invigorating because I saw that one need not be saved in order to be more Christ-like. At the core, however, I was a born-again Christian.

But I was teethering. Things happened. I saw how gentle the Arabs could be in Israel – in contrast to the Israelites. And then a rock concert in Lausanne lifted me more spiritually than anything that I had experienced in seminary.

We had bought a brand new Volkswagen for $1,300, and this gave us the freedom to go anywhere we wanted (we thought that gas was expensive at $3.00 a gallon).

We eventually made the decision to move to California. I wanted a high school job so that I could follow Dr. Keely's advice. However, most of the schools insisted that an applicant have a B-average to be considered as a candidate. That meant that I could only work at the college level.

While driving by a college, I stopped in to pick up an application. The president of the college happened to be walking by when I was talking about Danish folk high schools – schools for adults who want to improve their education for a five-month period. He had a great interest in this area and we had a nice conversation. He ended the conversation with the following, to a colleague:

Why don't you see if you can round up some of the English teachers? I'd like to see this man interviewed.

Thus, before we went to Europe, I had an interview with seven English teachers and eventually got a job at Grossmont College, which was fourteen miles from the Pacific Ocean. I remained at Grossmont College for ten years. During that time one might say that my faith was dwindling. So that I could also work with high school kids, I signed on as a Young Life counselor. Young Life is an organization that was a mixture of envangelical and non-evangelical high shool students. I became very close with all in the group, but I saw something that pushed me over the edge.

A retreat was going to be held at Big Bear Lake in the mountains of California. One of the non-Christian kids in the group didn't have enough money to be able to make it. What I saw amazed me. A group of non-evangelical boys and girls walked among the group asking for contributions so Paul could go to the retreat. It was their idea – not the evangelical kids. And it was the non-evangelical kids who contributed the most so that Paul could make it. This was an epiphany unto itself. From that point on I was no longer a religious person. This for me was the straw that broke the camel's back.

It is these epiphanies that make life so interesting. From that point on I was an agnostic. An agnostic is not an atheist but instead claims, "I don't have enough evidence to make a decision."

I believe in a Divine Creator, but not in the God mentioned in the Bible. That is simply too much for mankind (and womankind) to comprehend. Thus, as the writer of the *Past Shock* trilogy, I continue to have epiphanies and really enjoy life.

Appendix B

The Foundation of *Past Shock*

Close to 12,000 years ago a race of technically advanced beings was on this planet. According to best-selling researcher/author Zecheria Sitchin, these beings came here 400,000 years ago. Both mythology and holy books support this: more than 30,000 written documents tell of a group of advanced beings who either came to Earth or already were living on Earth. These documents—especially the Sumerian, Assyrian, and Babylonian writings—claim that these beings came to mine precious metals. Whether they came from outside the Earth or from another part of this planet is not really an important issue at this point. As the supply of precious metals began to deplete, the work became more demanding, and the miners became mutinous. The *Atra-hasis* is amazingly clear in this area:

> Let us confront our chief officer
> That he may relieve our heavy work...
> Excessive toil has killed us,
> Our work is heavy, the distress much.

In this amazingly complex work, the *Atra-hasis*—and many other "mythological" works—tells of long negotiations to prevent a bloody mutiny. Finally, the advanced beings decide on a solution to their problems:

> Let a Lulu (primitive worker) be created...
> While the Birth Goddess is present,
> Let her create a primitive worker.
> Let him bear the yoke...
> Let him carry the toil of the gods!
>
> *Atra-hasis*

Who was that primitive worker species? None other than what is today referred to as *Homo sapiens*. Yes, we are the species that was created to "do the toil of the gods."

111

What happened is the Annunaki (as the gods were called in the Babylonian, Assyrian, and Sumerian epics) crossed its genes with the genes of an animal that resembled them. That animal creature they used is what we now refer to as *Homo Neanderthalis* (Neanderthal Man). What the Annunaki created from Neanderthal was Cro-Magnon Man. For millions of years Neanderthal man had no written language or capacity for an elaborate vocabulary. Cro-Magnon man had this capacity almost immediately. Cro-Magnon Man was a genetic cross between the old level of man and the gods. If we had only been "good little workers" and stifled our god-like nature, we would not have brought down the wrath of the gods. However, something happened in this experiment that the gods were not counting on.

The Disastrous First Experiment

The genetic creation of humanity was not initially successful. Results were similar to the disastrous "killer bee" experiment performed in South America more than thirty years ago. The original intention of the scientists was to cross the genes of a stronger bee with the genes of a bee that was more prone to work harder. Instead, they created a very rebellious bee with killer instincts and a strong tendency to migrate. What the Annunaki wanted was a docile primitive worker who was smart enough to do menial work but not smart enough to discover that it was being exploited. Like the killer bee, *Homo sapiens* turned out to be very bright, innovative, and quite hostile to the idea of doing menial work. This initial group was bright—probably much brighter than we are now.

As a species we were so bright that we severely frightened our creators. They wanted us to do menial work in the mines, and we wanted to discover the secrets of the universe. If our creators had possessed a shred of spiritual evolvement, they would have nurtured us from our inception. However, their only intent was to exploit us. Thus, conflict erupted.

We rebelled against the idea of doing their dirty work. Eventually, they wanted us to fight wars for them, and we rebelled against that. This is clearly recorded in the *Old Testament,* other holy books, and in other ancient writings. This consistent theme runs through all of the past writings from all parts of the world. We were smart. Many of us may have been smarter than our own creators—and that must have severely frightened them. Then we started doing things that only increased their fears.

In *The Twelfth Planet* Zecheria Sitchin tells of a group of early humans in Babylonia that was so intelligent that it built a rocket ship capable of escaping the Earth's orbit. (Remember that the *Atra-hasis* and other ancient epics state that these gods claimed to come from the stars.) The gods were terrified that their newly created species might get back to the gods' homeland and tell of this infraction of the prime directive —not to interfere with any indigenous species. Thus, the gods got together and worked out a plan to prevent this:

> Come, let us go down and confound their language,
> that they might not understand one another's speech.
> (Genesis 11:7)

According to Sitchin, the above account is a more accurate version of the Tower of Babel story. Early humans were not building a tower as much as they were building a launching pad. Our getting free was something they could not allow, and they came down upon us brutally. Thus began the foundation of past shock.

ANOTHER VIEW OF THE GARDEN OF EDEN MYTH

What Really Happened at the Garden of Eden

Freud, Jung, and other founding fathers of psychology claim that even if the events of the Garden of Eden myth *didn't* happen, its impact as myth is still a gaping wound in our collective consciousness. Author Richard Heinberg in *Memories and Recollections of Paradise* relates how the human experience is shaped by our guilt for having been thrown out of the Garden of Eden. The consensus reality is that

God threw them out because they dared to eat of the Tree of Knowledge. It goes on to state that this was the beginning of sin and the point where the fall of man began. The problem with this consensus reality is that it is wrong. Instead, it was the beginning of a spiritual rape from which we are still shuddering (or at least blocking out).

Something did happen in the Garden of Eden—something very horrible. One of the gods, a pernicious pretender to divinity who called himself Yahweh (Jehovah), got totally caught up in his perverse paternalism and decided that Adam and Eve would be better off as cosmic, domesticated pets. The needs of these two people would be provided for as long as they remained at this level.

Adam and Eve were intelligent beings who were told to keep their lights under a bushel. Then, into the picture came a creature who thought Adam and Eve were getting a bad deal. Throughout history this creature has been greatly maligned. Some even claim that it was Lucifer, but not even the *Old Testament* calls him by that name. Instead, he is referred to as the Serpent. In most mythology and holy writings from throughout the world the Serpent is known as the purveyor of wisdom. For example, the Chinese saw both serpents and dragons as godlike, beneficial creatures who advanced humanity.

However, the Serpent has received very bad press from the Judeo-Christian segment of humanity. They saw—and continue to see—the serpent as evil, even as the devil. What the holy books do agree upon is that the serpent was very beautiful. Actually, it is amazing how much of the original story is left in the *Old Testament*.

Adam and Eve are told by Jehovah that they can have everything they want as long as they don't eat any fruit from the Tree of Knowledge. For them, this was equivalent to being told that you can have everything you want as long as you don't expect more than minimum wage and don't complain about the working conditions. They were told that if they ate of the fruit of the Tree of Knowledge, they would die.

This was a lie.

The Serpent appears and tells them that if they eat of the Tree of Knowledge their knowledge will increase significantly. At this point, the serpent is like Prometheus— about to steal fire from the gods and give it to humanity. Unlike Jehovah, the Serpent is telling the truth. His aim is not to destroy Adam and Eve as much as it is to liberate them.

What followed contributed greatly to past shock. Jehovah comes into the garden and says, "Where are you, Adam?" (something awfully strange to be stated by an omniscient God). Once Adam comes out of hiding, he observes a most traumatic event. Before Adam and Eve's eyes the Serpent is violently assaulted and mutilated—not something one would expect from an all-loving God, but unfortunately quite typical for the psychotic Jehovah. Other holy books describe an even more horrific fate for the Serpent: books like the *Jewish Pseudepigrapha* and *The Secret Book of John the Gnostic* tell of the Serpent brutally having each of its limbs hacked off and having to crawl on its belly from that time forth.

Then, of course, came all the other "prizes": women suffering in childbirth, men having to work by the sweat of their brow, and other multiplications of sorrow and pain. This was not the act of a loving god; this was the heinous act of a mentally tortured warlord who dared to tell his new "creations" that he was God. This expulsion from paradise was traumatic; however, it was also the beginning of humanity's liberation. (Ken Wilber's excellent book *Up From Eden* effectively discusses this thesis. Rollo May also touches upon this thesis in *The Courage to Create*.)

BACK TO THE DRAWING BOARDS

The Spiritual Rape Intensifies

One theme stands out in the thousands of mythological and holy writings: our creators did not like the way they originally created us. We were too smart and—from their perspective—too arrogant. We refused to become domesticated and we complained incessantly. The *Atra-hasis* tells of one of the gods who had enough:

The god Enlil said to the other gods:

> Oppressive have become the pronouncements
> of Mankind. Their conjugations deprive me of
> sleep.
>
> *Atra-hasis*

Being old enough to have suffered through three years of Latin studies, this writer finds perverse humor in this. However, Enlil (whom many claimed was Jehovah) sees no humor in the wailing pronouncements of his newly created worker race. Something had to be done. A new creation was needed: a dumbed-down worker human. They had already created spiritual rape by advancing us too quickly; now they were going to "de-advance" us.

The gods were mentally imbalanced Rodney Dangerfields who felt they just didn't get enough respect. Not only did they want workers who didn't complain, they also wanted us to venerate and revere them. While this is also a dominant theme in ancient writings, the one that best describes this "dumbing down" is the Mayan *Popul Vuh*. This holy book not only tells how the gods created humans as a work force, but also how they had to keep recreating humanity:

> We have already tried with our first creations,
> our first creations, our first creatures, but
> we could not make them praise and venerate us.

> So let us try to create obedient, respectful
> beings who will nourish and respect us.
>
> —*Popul Vuh*

Writing this off as "merely mythology" may create a seemingly safe certainty. However, it also keeps humans in a state of denial about what really happened to them in the past. Could it be that we turned out to be more intelligent than our creators? Is it possible that we were brutally treated because we refused to act like domesticated beasts of burden? According to the *Popul Vuh,* the dumbing down worked (in this case after five previous, ineffective experiments). What exactly was it that they were trying to dumb down?

> They saw and they instantly could see far,
> they succeeded in seeing, they succeeded in
> knowing where all is in the world. When they
> looked, they saw instantly all around them,
> and they contemplated in turn the arch of the
> heaven and the round face of the earth.
>
> —*Popul Vuh*

This is what had to be dumbed down. This is what frightened our creators. This was one of the most heinous acts of our misguided creators. We were genetically engineered and conditioned from birth to be creatures that would venerate and worship those who "created"—and spiritually raped—us. The *Popul Vuh* states how the gods were finally "victorious" in making us obedient workers who worshipped our genetic creators as if they were the creators of the universe and the creators of the soul.

In actuality, they were liars who were bored and used us as play fodder. They demanded worship because their souls were undeveloped. They made us fight their wars because they lacked the resolve and courage to fight them on their own. They made us build large edifices to praise them when they weren't even close to being worthy of our praise. We believed all of this because we had been so dumbed

down that we no longer had the capacity to question those who committed this spiritual tyranny. We worshipped them because they treated us quite brutally if we didn't. We fought their wars because we
knew that we would be slaughtered if we didn't. We praised them
because that was what they wanted, and they got quite nasty if they
didn't get their way.

With every veneration and praise, we etched the cellular conditioning that these pretenders were God. We must have known that
this was a sham because we resisted valiantly. Jehovah kept the
Israelites in the wilderness for forty years so that he could have a third
generation of killer warriors. He didn't want a complaining Moses, nor
a questioning Aaron. After forty years he had Joshua who moved—and
destroyed—without question. The violation of another people's sovereignty wasn't even questioned. Pretender god Jehovah ordained it, and
the highly conditioned Israelites marched forward in their slaughter.

In the *Bhagavad Gita,* the warrior Arjuna wants to work out a
peace with his enemies. However, Krishna at first persuades and then
eventually goads Arjuna into fighting. How amazing that very few
people are willing to see Krishna as the warmonger and Arjuna as the
willing peacemaker. Because Krishna is seen as a God, most who read
this account figure that he must have been right.

He wasn't. He was a technologically advanced being who was
only interested in overcoming boredom and conquering territory. He
didn't care the slightest bit about the development of Arjuna's soul.

One only need look as far as the *Old Testament* to see an example of a god meddling in the process of peacemaking. Moses and
Pharaoh had worked out a separate peace, but Jehovah would have
none of it. He wanted slaughter—and most likely good theater. He
wanted it so badly that he told Moses that he (Jehovah) had hardened
Pharaoh's heart so that he might do battle. This, of course, led to the
Red Sea slaughter that, according to one of David's Psalms, killed
many on both sides. Yet Moses and Pharaoh had worked it out so this

would have to happen. Jehovah probably needed a way to get his Israelites into the desert so that he could whip them into shape and make sure that no peacemakers ever messed with his plans again.

This is rape—spiritual and physical. The conditioning has etched itself so deeply into our cellular memory that the slaughtering by the Serbs in Bosnia and the outrageous genocide in Darfur, Sudan seem more like natural reflexes than horrific acts. The massacre of 6,000,000 Jews was an easy process. The Christians in the area smelled the bodies burning, but they could not or would not resist. This comes as much from war conditioning as slave conditioning.

These "wonderful" gods beat us into submission if we dared to move out of our "slave chip" paradigm. 5,000 years later, when the escape from the Sobibor concentration camp began (with most of the SS officers already killed), many could not run to their freedom. Many simply stood with heads bowed and prayed instead of running. Now that's powerful conditioning—conditioning that began 5,000 to 10,000 years ago and continues today like a slave chip playing repeatedly in our brains.

What could they do to us then that caused us to be like this now?

AN OFFER YOU BETTER NOT REFUSE

Jehovah's Devastating Covenant

Anyone reading Jehovah's words out of the context of the *Old Testament* would conclude that these were either the words of a raving lunatic or the ramblings of someone no longer grounded in reality.

> If you follow my laws and faithfully observe
> my commandments, I will grant you rains
> in their season so that the earth shall yield
> its produce and the trees of the field their

fruit. Your threshing shall overtake the vintage,
and the vintage shall overtake the sowing;
you shall eat your fill of bread and dwell
securely in your land.

I will grant peace in the land, and you will
lie down untroubled by anyone; I will give the
land respite from vicious beasts, and no sword
shall cross your land. You shall give chase to
your enemies, and they shall fall before you by
the sword...

I will look with favor upon you, and make you
fertile and multiply you; and I will maintain
my covenant with you. You shall eat grain
long stored...

(Leviticus 26:3-10)

These are the words of Yahweh/Jehovah to the Israelites. Sounds like a fair deal... right? Think for a moment about this. Consider that you own a thriving business; you are doing quite well on your own business initiative. In comes a well-dressed character and says, "I have a deal for you. If you will pay me $3,000 a month, I will make sure that your business continues to be successful."

You mention that your business is doing quite well on its own and that you don't need help from anyone.

Then the man leans closer to you and says, "You don't understand. If you don't pay us the $3,000 each month, we're going to stand outside your door and tell people that we've been cheated. We're going to tell people that you won't honor your commitments and that your merchandise will break down within weeks. We're going to tell people that you're planning to go out of business and that your customers will be stuck with your product."

Immediately, you recognize the protection racket. These people are simply protecting you from the wrath that they intend to wreak upon you. You are gaining nothing, but instead have to pay for things to remain the same.

What does this have to do with Jehovah? Read on:

> But if you do not obey me and do not observe
> these commandments, if you reject my laws and
> spurn my norms, so that you do not observe
> all of my commandments and you break my
> Covenant, I in turn will do this to you. I will
> wreak misery upon you—consumption and fever,
> which cause the eyes to pine and the body to
> languish; you shall sow your seed to no purpose,
> for your enemies shall eat it. I will set my face
> against you; you shall be routed by your enemies,
> and your foes shall dominate you. You shall flee
> though none pursues.
>
> (Leviticus 26:14-17)

This is not a loving God who cares for his children. This is instead a highly manipulative warlord claiming to be God—a pretender to the throne. This is a petty entity, incapable of gentle persuasion, who is spiritually raping the people he claims to love.

But hang on, it gets "better":

> And if for all that you do not obey me, I will
> go on disciplining you sevenfold for your sins,
> and I will break your proud glory. I will make
> the skies like iron and your earth like copper,
> so that your strength shall be spent to no
> purpose. Your land shall not yield its produce,
> nor shall the trees of it yield their fruit.
>
> (Leviticus 26:18-20)

Sevenfold for your sins... isn't that a bit excessive? What happened to an eye for an eye? This is seven days of detention for an offense requiring one day. This is swatting a dog on seven different occasions for defecating once on the rug. Plain and simply put, this is cruel and unusual punishment—the kind of punishment meted out by vengeful people set on effecting a vendetta. Yet few—even in the Mafia—would mete out a seven-fold vendetta. This is the pronouncement of a very sick mind. Yet Jehovah told the Israelites that he was God—the only God worthy of being worshipped. By his very actions this pretender god was worthy of nothing but our contempt.

However, this "deal" that Jehovah is forcing on his people gets even worse:

> And if for all that, you do not obey me,
> I will go on disciplining you seven fold
> for your sins. I will loose wild beasts
> against you, and they shall bereave you
> of your children, and wipe out your cattle...
>
> ...and if you withdraw into your cities, I
> will send pestilence among you, and you
> shall be delivered into enemy hands....
> You shall eat the flesh of your sons and
> the flesh of your daughters.... I will heap
> your carcasses on your lifeless fetishes.
>
> I will spurn you. I will lay your cities in
> ruin and make your sanctuaries desolate....
> And you will scatter among nations, and I
> will unsheathe the sword against you. Your
> land shall become a desolation and your
> cities a ruin.
>
> (Leviticus 26:21-33)

Christian O'Brien, author of *The Genius of the Few,* claims that this covenant was disturbing for four reasons: (1) it was not a freely negotiated agreement between both parties; (2) the punishments proposed were not even close to being civilized; (3) people other than the offenders would be punished—the good would have to suffer along with the bad; (4) sin was being returned with evil—the punishment went far beyond the elements of the "crime."

However, understanding the dark side of Jehovah is essential. This is the entity who ordered a man stoned to death for picking up sticks on the Sabbath. This is the entity who threw poisonous snakes into a crowd of people—and killed many of them—simply because they were complaining. This is the entity who beamed with joy when he was told that one of his follower had impaled someone because he was not following the commandments.

This is also the entity who—despite claiming to be omnipotent—warned only a few people of an impending natural disaster and watched from above as millions of his creations died a terrifying death by drowning. This is the entity that a majority of Americans worship as the God of the Christians and Jews.

This is also the god who spiritually raped us—his new creations—and created a past shock that lies deep within each and every one of us. This is the entity who insured that we would continue to worship him long after he departed. Exactly how did he do that? He and his cohorts designed a system of conditioning so effective that its devastating impact remains even today. What these pretender gods created in order to keep us in line was religion.

THE ORIGINS OF RELIGION

Conditioning the New Creations to Be Spiritual Slaves

For just a couple of minutes, assume that you are very high up in the ranks of these pretender gods. You created humans as a slave race—a herd to do your dirty work. With extended leisure time, you decided that you needed some warriors to help you conquer lands from the other entities that were mining the planet. When these chess-like battles became boring, you decided that you needed some entertainment—something more like theater.

But for now, the warriors are refusing to fight—or play their proper roles. The workers are refusing to work and are expending their energies, instead, in rioting. Also—God forbid—many who are realizing that their lives don't show much promise are committing suicide. Just how do you make sure that your new creations fight your wars, do your dirty work, and stop committing suicide? After much discussion among the ranks, you finally come to an answer: create a religion.

In this religion you promise rewards in the next life—for eternity—as long as your creations play *your* game in this life. Not theirs. This means sweating and toiling without rebellion. It also means worshipping those who created you. For those who are just a tad unimpressed, you invent another place called Hell, which promises great misery for eternity if your laws are not kept. To insure that they continue fighting for you, you promise that dying in war is an automatic ticket to heaven.

Additionally, those who commit suicide automatically go to hell. This insures that those humans who get depressed with their lot will remain with that lot, stuck fast in the hope that they will get to rest for eternity. In an attempt to secure an eternity in Paradise, these badly conditioned and spiritually raped humans will spend their free time worshipping the creators and bending to their every whim. Because they have successfully blocked any memory of the spiritual realms— and all memory of past lives—these newly created humans have no way to prove whether this religion is real or false. Since religion deals in eternities, one quickly realizes that it is best to play the game of the pretender gods.

Being one of these pretender gods, you had to be rock sure that your creations played your game according to your rules. To achieve this surety, you create the ultimate cosmic "good cop/bad cop" game. You construct a personal embodiment of a force that is trying to keep your creations in a state of sin (wanting to worship other gods, not obeying the dictates of the gods, not wanting to work, lusting after other women, etc.). You claim that this other entity wants their souls and that, if this entity succeeds, they will spend all of eternity in hell. Thus, when you are told by one of these humans that he feels he is being exploited or that he wants to make peace with his enemies, you can tell him that this is the evil one working in his life. He should pray to be guided by the forces of righteousness (that being you).

What is interesting in all this is that when any of your rebellious forces experience pangs of conscience for what you are doing to them, you can condition them into believing that those who want to liberate them are evil. This is what happened with the Serpent in the Garden of Eden. This is what happened with Prometheus when he stole fire from the gods and gave it to humanity. This is what happened with the Norse god Loki who tried to throw a "monkey wrench" into the slave conditioning of the gods and, according to the legend, made things so unbearable for them that they finally left.

The pretender gods themselves may have left, but their conditioning remains. Inside each and every one of us is a slave chip that continues the conditioning of these despicable beings. This slave chip is the result of many genetic experiments and thousands of years of religious conditioning. We follow that conditioning today as if these pretender gods were still in our midst. The singer of the song might be gone, but the melody lingers on with a devastating impact.

During the Korean War a soldier was told to guard a certain area until he was relieved. However, unbeknownst to the soldier, during his time at post the enemy had wiped out the squad he was guarding. Thus, for three days he continued to guard the area. Finally, sometime into the fourth day he collapsed from exhaustion and slept. When he woke up, he felt tremendous guilt that he had fallen asleep. He had no way of knowing that no one could have possibly relieved him. So he continued in his guilt, believing that it was his fault that all of his squadron was killed.

Humanity is collectively like that soldier. As early humans, we were conditioned to worship interlopers and pretenders as God. These pretenders deserted us and left us to our own resources to survive because they no longer had need of us. However, that awesome and devastating conditioning remains with us, and we stay at our "post". Like sheep, we continue the patterns of worship. We still offer our bodies to fight the holy wars—and have hopes of paradise for participating in the slaughter.

Our world of work is still not structured to serve the worker; instead, god-like "superiors" are paid much more than they are worth because they can easily find worker drones who will work for much less than they are worth. We are so well conditioned that most any movement toward spiritual liberation will create guilt and a feeling that one is falling from the fold. We have been programmed well. We feel spiritually nourished to the degree that we remain as spiritual slaves.

With no guidance from the pretender gods—or God himself, we burned brilliant people like John Hus and Giordano Bruno at the stake, threatened Galileo with brutal torture, and were able to free captured hostages from the embassy of "The Great Satan" in Iran. All in the name of Christ, humans have slaughtered whole cities, raped and massacred the Indians we were trying to convert, and held heresy trails and painful executions for those who dared not believe. We continue to sing praises to a long gone force "which saved a wretch like me." We see ourselves as sin-bound creatures. Those who "refuse" to see in such a light still suffer from the dumbing down of the pretender gods. We walk this planet with a brain that is capable of moving mountains, yet we still use very little of it.

We are victims of a long-past spiritual rape that had made past shock a part of our experience. The more we are willing to face what actually happened in our past, the more that we will be able to overcome this past shock and begin living as the humans that we are capable of becoming. The time to begin this exploration is now.

Past Shock: The Origin of Religion and Its Impact on the Human Soul. Part One.

This book reveals the true reasons why religion was created, what organized religion won't tell you, the reality of the "slave chip" programming we all have to deal with, why we had to be created over and over again, what really happened in the Garden of Eden, what the Tower of Babel was and the reason why we were stopped from building it, how we were conditioned to remain spiritually ignorant, and much more. Jack exposes what he calls the "pretender gods," advanced beings who were not divine, but had knowledge of scientific principles, including genetic engineering. Our advanced science of today has unraveled their secrets, and Jack Barranger has the knowledge and courage to expose exactly how we were manipulated.

ISBN 978-1-885395-085 • 132 pages • $12.95

The Origin of Religion and Its Impact on the Human Soul: Past Shock Part Two

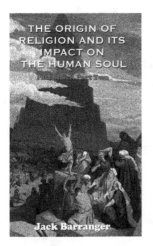

Who were the ancient gods and why did they come here? Historical evidence shows that we worked for them and tried to appease them at every turn. Then, at some point, they left. Cultures from around the world tell their stories through mythology and they are still worshipped in our religions. Their power over us was so strong that it is still with us today. We have been conditioned in a religious way and Barranger shows how this conditioning is, in certain ways, stunting our spiritual growth. The author reveals exactly how this "slave chip" from the gods has programmed us, and how we can finally break free.

ISBN 978-1-58509-113-3 • 149 pages • $15.95